The Perennial Way

Expanded Edition

The Perennial Way
Expanded Edition

Yoga Sutras
Ashtavakra Gita
Dhammapada
Book of Yeshua
Heart Sutra
Three Books of the Absolute
Avadhuta Gita
Faith Mind Sutra
Atma Shatakam
Tao Te Ching

Bart Marshall

REALFACE PRESS

BOOKS PUBLISHED BY REALFACE PRESS

Holy Bible: King James Reader's Version, translated by Bart Marshall

Christ Sutras: The Complete Sayings of Jesus from All Sources Arranged into Sermons, compiled and composed by Bart Marshall

The Perennial Way (Expanded Edition), translated by Bart Marshall

Letters of Transmission: The Enlightenment Method of Zen Master Alfred Pulyan, edited by Bart Marshall

The Emerald Tablets of Thoth the Atlantean, edited by Bart Marshall

Bhagavad Gita, translated by Bart Marshall

Ashtavakra Gita: Dialogues on Self-Realization, translated by Bart Marshall

Dhammapada: The Sayings of Gotama Buddha, translated by Bart Marshall

Tao Te Ching: The Sayings of Lao Tsu, translated by Bart Marshall

Yoga Sutras of Patanjali: Meditation Edition, translated by Bart Marshall

Avadhuta Gita: Song of the Ever-Free, translated by Bart Marshall

Contents

Preface to the Expanded Edition

In the years since publication of *The Perennial Way*, I've been humbled and gratified by the reception it has received, and by the wonderful comments from readers about the essential place it has found in their lives and search for Truth.

I have also received suggestions about other spiritual works readers would like me to tackle in a similar way, most often the *Bhagavad Gita*, which I have since published separately, and also two lesser known Advaita classics, *Avadhuta Gita* and *Atma Shatakam*, which I've included in this edition.

I've also included two other works, *Three Books of the Absolute*, and *Book of Yeshua*. *Three Books of the Absolute* is an epic poem by the modern mystic Richard Rose that dramatically describes his Realization and what was realized.

Book of Yeshua contains selected sayings of Jesus of Nazareth, who's name in his native language of Aramaic, is Yeshua. It is excerpted from my book *Christ Sutras: The Complete Sayings of Jesus from All Sources Arranged as Sermons*, and conveys the inner teachings of Jesus in his own words, teachings that are very similar to those of Advaita, Buddhism, Zen, and the other traditions anthologized here.

Readers have also asked why I haven't written about the similarities between all these great teachings and provided more commentary in the introductions. My feeling is that commentary often gets in the way of a reader's direct communion with the masters, and my intention with these translations is that they speak clearly and directly for themselves, with a powerful self-evidence that needs no commentary.

Better for you to discover for yourself the similarities between Jesus and Lao Tsu, than for me or anyone else to point them out. Better for you to be caught off-guard and struck speechless by a profound verse in *Ashtavakra Gita*, than for me or anyone else to tell you what to feel or hear in it—or worse, how to "understand" it.

There is nothing in these spiritual masterworks that you don't already know in the deep recesses of your heart and soul. Reading them is a journey into Self. Have at it, and Godspeed.

Introduction

In Vietnam when I was twenty-one a hand grenade or mortar round—circumstances made it difficult to determine which—blew me into a clear and brilliant blackness that felt like "Home." For the next thirty-seven years that glimpse of infinite, intimate emptiness kept me looking almost obsessively in esoteric books, far corners, and inner reaches for an explanation of myself. Finally, at the age of fifty-eight, the veil "suddenly" lifted.

After a few weeks of blissful aftershock, life resumed. At the spiritual self-inquiry group I'd been attending, friends naturally had questions. I found myself tongue-tied trying to answer. I struggled for words, or just stared ahead, choked up. The capacity to communicate does not come with the experience.

For several months after the occurrence I had no interest in reading—or most anything else for that matter—but when I did start to pick up books again I found myself drawn mainly to the old masters. How did Buddha talk about This? How did Lao Tsu? Jesus? Patanjali? I read them with new eyes.

Oddly, in all those years of seeking I had never read the *Ashtavakra Gita*. But a year after seeking ended, at the bedside of my dying teacher, a friend placed it in my hands. I opened it and was astonished. Here, in one small book, was everything that needed to be said. Rather than stumble over my own words from now on I could just hand out copies and say, "Here, read this."

At the same time, however, I was struck by the degree to which the language of the translation got in the way, how it obscured as much as it illuminated. I acquired all the other versions I could find and compared them, looking for the best. Literal transcriptions were valuable as reference, but required patient study to understand. English translations by Indian scholars made the meaning more clear, but tended to lack a certain rhythm and nuance of language I sensed in the original. Translations by native English speakers were better in this regard, but more likely to de-fang the teachings or just plain miss the point.

Somewhere along the way I realized I was "hearing" what I thought to be the clearest, most direct, most faithful translation of a verse and judging the others by it. I started writing down what I heard.

The process was infectious. When *Ashtavakra Gita* was completed, I just kept going. *Tao Te Ching* came next, the first spiritual text to have a major impact on me as I began searching for answers, and perhaps one reason I later took Chinese as my language in college. I can no longer read Chinese, though, nor can I read Pali, or Sanskrit. I wish I could. It would be great to read these works as written. I found, though, that by studying and comparing a variety of English translations, as well as literal transcriptions and dictionaries, I was able to triangulate and "reverse engineer" back to the words and intention of the masters, then build back up again into what seemed (to me at least) the clearest, most faithful expression of the original.

    Yoga Sutras, Dhammapada, Heart Sutra, Ashtavakra Gita, Faith Mind Sutra, and *Tao Te Ching* are considered by many to be the essential statements of Yoga, Buddhism, Advaita, Taoism, and Ch'an (Zen). It is to these traditions that serious seekers of enlightenment are generally drawn because they form the core methodology of a teaching we might call (to borrow from Huxley) the Perennial Way.

    The Perennial Way points to something that cannot be seen, experienced, or spoken—call it God, Tao, One, Absolute—and says it is possible to know It directly, to realize It as your true Self. The Way is not about beliefs or understanding. It's not ancient, not something to be studied like history or religion. What it points to is ever-present—the Source of all that is. It speaks through those who enter It to anyone who'll listen and says, "Come home."

    In the verses that follow, Patanjali, Buddha, Jesus, Lao Tsu, and other great masters of the Way speak with resonant authority on man's deepest questions, and offer explicit instructions for how an earnest seeker of Truth should conduct his or her search and life.

Oxherding Picture One: In Search of the Bull

In the pasture of this world, I endlessly push aside the tall grasses
in search of the bull. Following unnamed rivers,
lost upon the interpenetrating paths of distant mountains,
my strength failing and my vitality exhausted, I cannot find the bull.
I only hear the locusts chirring through the forest at night.

The bull is not lost. What need is there to search?
Only because of separation from my true nature do I fail to see him.
In the confusion of the senses I lose even his tracks.
Far from home, I see many crossroads, but know not where to turn.
Greed and fear, good and bad, entangle me.

Oxherding Picture Two: Discovering the Footprints

Along the riverbank under the trees, I discover footprints!
Even under the fragrant grass I see his prints.
Deep in remote mountains they are found.
These traces no more can be hidden than one's nose, looking heavenward.

Understanding the teaching, I see the footprints of the bull.
I learn that just as many utensils are made from one metal,
so too are the myriad entities made of the fabric of Self.
Unless I discriminate, how will I perceive the true from the untrue?
Not yet having entered the gate, nevertheless I have discerned the path.

[In the Zen tradition, the Ten Oxherding Pictures depict the stages of the path to enlightenment. Pictures 3 – 10 appear elsewhere in this book.]

Yoga Sutras

Patanjali

The *Yoga Sutras of Patanjali* were written around the time of Jesus, give or take 200 years. The practice of yoga began in India as early as 1000 years prior, but the *Yoga Sutras* are the most important compendium of this ancient oral tradition, and virtually all later schools of yoga begin with Patanjali.

Little is known about him, but there is evidence he was an educated philosopher, grammarian, and physician—a long-lost medical work is attributed to him. No doubt he received oral instruction in yoga and probably lived in mountain caves and forests, or along river banks—the most common practicing grounds of the time. At some point, enlightenment happened.

Why he committed an oral tradition to written text is unknown, but as the remote meditative havens of the yogis receded and dedicated aspirants dwindled, he may have feared that yoga would become forgotten, lost or corrupted. Regardless, we are the beneficiaries of his efforts.

The literal meaning of the word *sutra* is "thread," which by extension and usage has come to connote "spiritual instruction." Simple, direct, practical—yet not necessarily easy to understand or practice—the threads of Patanjali weave an elegant system for opening the way to Self-realization.

1. Unity

OM. What follows are instructions on Unity.   1.1

Unity obtains when the activities of mind have ceased.   1.2

The witness then abides in its true nature.   1.3

Otherwise, the witness is identified with the activities of mind   1.4
and is just another thought-form itself.

There are five types of mind activity,   1.5
both painful and pleasurable.

These are: correct perception, misperception,   1.6
imagination, dreamless sleep, and memory.

Correct perception may derive from direct observation,   1.7
valid reasoning, or accurate testimony of enlightened teachers.

Misperception is knowledge based on the illusion of forms,   1.8
rather than on the true nature of reality.

Imagination is mental images derived from words and concepts   1.9
rather than objective observation and sensory perceptions.

Dreamless sleep is the state of mind when thought is absent   1.10
and sensory perception is in abeyance.

Memory is the retention of thoughts and images generated   1.11
by sensory perception and imagination.

Cessation of mind activity is achieved through the practice   1.12
of yoga and the habit of dispassionate non-attachment.

Yoga practice is the willful effort to restrain the five activities   1.13
of mind and abide in a state of stillness.

To be firmly grounded, this practice must be performed   1.14
with earnestness and devotion over a long period of time,
all the while holding the goal in clear and constant view.

Dispassionate non-attachment is the absence of desire for   1.15
experiences of the senses — seen and unseen, here and hereafter.

Supreme dispassion is indifference to the three *gunas*   1.16
of creation — light, inertia, and vibration —
owing to a direct knowledge of Self.

Meditation for direct-knowing of the objective world   1.17
is fourfold in nature: exterior observation, inner perception,
alert stillness, and the sense "I am."

The other state of meditation is when awareness perceives no   1.18
thought or object — only the seeds of unmanifested possibilities.

This is the natural state of formless beings   1.19
and those absorbed in True Nature.

Others can attain it through faith, earnestness,   1.20
self-inquiry, clarity, and insight.

Those who proceed with unshakable intent   1.21
can attain this state quickly.

Those who practice with varying degrees of effort —   1.22
mild, moderate, intense — will succeed
in accordance with their efforts.

The other way to attain the natural state   1.23
is through surrender to God.

God is the Supreme Being, formless, unbounded,   1.24
limitless, untouched by action and desire.

The omniscience of God is infinite.   1.25
Man has but a germ of awareness.

God is timeless, the ever-present master of the ancient masters. 1.26

He is called by OM. 1.27

Silently repeat this word as a mantra 1.28
while meditating upon its significance.

From this comes the disappearance of obstacles 1.29
to the realization of Self.

The obstacles to Self-realization are disease, inertia, doubt, 1.30
carelessness, procrastination, laziness, sense cravings,
false perception, inability to concentrate,
and inability to stabilize higher states when attained.

Encountering these obstacles one experiences grief, 1.31
despair, physical agitation and anxious breathing.

To overcome these obstacles, the constant practice 1.32
of a single truth is required.

The mind can be stilled by the earnest practice of openness, 1.33
compassion, virtue, and indifference.

Or by breathing in and out, intentionally. 1.34

Intentional focus on any sense experience 1.35
will enhance perception and still the mind.

Concentration upon the inner light beyond sorrow 1.36
stills the mind.

Meditation upon a transcendent being stills the mind. 1.37

Inquiring into the experiences of dreams and dreamless sleep 1.38
stills the mind.

Fixing attention on that which is nearest the heart, 1.39
also stills the mind.

The stilled mind of a yoga master realizes everything,   1.40
from the infinitely small to the infinitely great.

As pure crystal takes on the adjacent colors,   1.41
so does the mind free of thought become indistinguishable
from that which it contemplates. The perceiver,
the experience of perceiving, and the object perceived are one.

When the mind projects names and concepts on what is seen   1.42
through direct perception, confusion and delusion result.

When the mind is clear, empty of memories and knowledge,   1.43
things are seen exactly as they are.

These same two conditions — projection and clarity —   1.44
also apply to the perception of subtle, unmanifest realms.

The observation of progressively more subtle realms   1.45
leads to the primal source.

All these meditations have separate perceptions as their seed.   1.46

When there is no perception of separateness,   1.47
the supreme Self reigns.

And absolute Truth is revealed as self-evident.   1.48

The direct experience of Truth is nothing like intellectual   1.49
knowledge gained from scriptures and teachings.

The direct experience of Truth supersedes and destroys   1.50
all previous impressions.

When the impression of a direct experience of Truth   1.51
is also wiped out, there remains only Awareness without seed.

2. Practice

Purification, self-inquiry, and surrender to God
are the practices that lead to Unity. 2.1

These practices cultivate awareness and remove the afflictions
that obstruct realization of Truth. 2.2

The obstructing afflictions are ignorance, false sense of self,
desire, aversion, and a tenacious clinging to life. 2.3

Ignorance is the origin of all other afflictions — the pre-emergent
and the vestigial, the nearly-overcome and the fully operational. 2.4

Ignorance regards the impermanent as permanent,
the impure as pure, the bad as good, the ego self as True Self. 2.5

The false ego self is born when the instrument of seeing
is misidentified as being separate from the One that sees. 2.6

Desire is attachment to pleasure. 2.7

Aversion is attachment to the absence of suffering. 2.8

Tenacious clinging to life is inherent in all beings,
from the most ignorant to the most wise.
Life after life, it is sustained by its own momentum. 2.9

When these five afflictions have become subtle, vestigial,
they can be destroyed by abiding in their opposites. 2.10

When they are fully operational, they must be overcome
through meditation. 2.11

Mental and physical actions rooted in these afflictions bear fruit
as experiences in this and future lifetimes. 2.12

For so long as the roots exist, they bear fruit as fortune of birth,
length of life, and the experience of pleasure or suffering. 2.13

The pleasure or suffering you experience is the fruit of your   2.14
good or bad actions.

One who is spiritually aware sees that all experience   2.15
is suffering, due to constant change, anxiety,
forces of nature, and imprints of subliminal processes.

Suffering yet to come can be avoided.   2.16

Suffering is caused by the illusion that there is an experiencer   2.17
to whom an experience is happening.

Everything perceived is composed of the three gunas   2.18
of creation—light, inertia, and vibration. These form
the elements as well as the senses, which interact to create
experience and the path to liberation from it.

The three gunas flow in four states—   2.19
gross, subtle, primal, and unmanifest.

The witness is Self—pure Awareness—   2.20
which, though boundless and unchanging,
appears to perceive the world through the construct of mind.

The existence of *All That Is*, serves Self-Awareness alone.   2.21

One who attains Unity sees the world is not real,   2.22
yet the world persists because it is taken by others as real.

The identification of pure Awareness with the mind   2.23
and the creations of the mind causes the apprehension
of both an objective world and a perceiver of it.

This identification is ignorance. It must be overcome.   2.24

When this identification is broken, ignorance vanishes,   2.25
liberation is attained, and Self realizes its true nature.

Liberation is attained through unwavering intent
and discernment.   2.26

The way of Self-realization progresses through seven stages.   2.27

Steady practice of the means of yoga dissolves impurities
and invites illumination of the Real.   2.28

The eight means of yoga are self-restraint, faithful observance,
right posture, intentional breathing, sense withdrawal,
concentration, meditation, and awareness.   2.29

The five pillars of self-restraint are non-violence,
truthfulness, honesty, celibacy, and non-attachment.   2.30

These great practices are valid for all—
irrespective of social class, location, time, or circumstance—
and thus constitute the universal Way.   2.31

The five observances are purification, contentment,
aspiration, study, and surrender to God.   2.32

To be free of thoughts contrary to yoga,
opposite thoughts must be cultivated.   2.33

Contrary thoughts leading to acts of violence, dishonesty
and lust—whether personally done, caused to be done,
or merely approved of—arise from greed, anger, and ignorance.
And whether mild, moderate, or intense,
they perpetuate suffering and delusion.
This is why their opposites must be cultivated.   2.34

In the presence of one who is grounded in non-violence,
enmity is not possible.   2.35

When one is obedient to Truth,
what he says and does becomes what is true.   2.36

When one is established in non-stealing, wealth flows to him.   2.37

One who is steadfast in celibacy acquires spiritual energy,
strength, and courage.

2.38

One who is unattached and free of cravings
gains insight into all of life — past, present, and yet to come.

2.39

Physical and mental purification produces an indifference
to one's own body, and ends one's infatuation
with the bodies of others.

2.40

One who is pure of heart obtains serenity of spirit,
power of concentration, control of the senses,
and the capacity to directly realize Self.

2.41

Through contentment one attains bliss.

2.42

The fire of aspiration burns through impurities
and heightens the powers of the body and senses.

2.43

Through self-inquiry and spiritual study
one attains communion with the object of study.

2.44

Through surrender to God one realizes clear Awareness.

2.45

Right posture is to be seated in a manner both solid and relaxed.

2.46

Effortless stillness is achieved by focusing the mind
on the boundless realm.

2.47

Here, the opposites hold no sway.

2.48

When right posture is attained,
the practice of intentional breathing then follows.

2.49

Intentional breathing controls the three phases of breath —
exhalation, inhalation, and hiatus.
Breathing can be regulated by controlling the spacing,
depth, number, and duration of breaths.

2.50

There is a fourth level of breath so subtle it transcends
the realm of internal and external sense objects.

Through these practices the veil that obscures
the inner light is lifted.

And the mind becomes capable of concentrating attention.

When the mind withdraws attention from sense experience,
the senses receive no impressions from sense objects,
and awareness rests in its essential nature.

In this way, complete mastery of the senses is achieved.

2.51

2.52

2.53

2.54

2.55

3. Powers

Concentration is the unwavering focus of attention
on a single object in consciousness. 3.1

Meditation is the effortless flow of sustained concentration. 3.2

Reflection is when objects in consciousness
are directly experienced as they are, free of mind,
with no degree of separation. 3.3

Concentration, meditation, reflection.
These three constitute *samyama* — detached awareness. 3.4

Through mastery of samyama,
the essence of wisdom is illuminated. 3.5

It is applied in stages. 3.6

The three aspects of samyama are more intimate and internal
than are the five self-restraints previously described. 3.7

But even these are external to the seedless absorption of *samadhi*. 3.8

Thoughts arise from no-thought, play out, then vanish.
In the emptiness between thoughts,
the mind is capable of self-reflection. 3.9

When thought is absent, the flow of mind is stilled. 3.10

When mental distractions disappear,
what remains is one-pointed awareness. 3.11

One-pointedness is when the arising thought
and the vanishing thought are the same — with no gap between. 3.12

In this state, the mind passes beyond the realm of forms
and sense organs — beyond observation of attributes,
ideas of purpose, and perception of apparent change. 3.13

16

The three properties of specific forms are:
potential characteristics, manifest characteristics,
and the unmanifest source common to all forms.

3.14

The interplay of these three properties
creates the appearance of evolutionary change.

3.15

The practice of samyama on the triple-nature of specific forms
leads to an understanding of past and future manifestations.

3.16

The sound of a word, the object it denotes, and the thought
conjured up by the word are confused by the ordinary mind
as being the same. By practicing samyama on the distinction
between these, the yogi comes to understand the meaning
of sounds made by all living things.

3.17

By practicing samyama on the flow of thought-images,
knowledge of previous existence arises.

3.18

By practicing samyama on others,
knowledge of their thoughts arises.

3.19

However, the object of another's thoughts —
being distinct from the thought itself —
cannot be known by the practice of samyama.

3.20

By practicing samyama on the essential nature of his own form,
the yogi gains control over the emanations
that make his body visible to others.

3.21

In this way also, he gains control of the emanations of sound,
smell, and substance of his body,
and can thus vanish completely from the senses of others.

3.22

Some actions in life bear fruit quickly. Others ripen late.
By practicing samyama on the karma of his life,
a yogi comes to know the exact time it will end.
This can also be known through signs and omens.

3.23

By practicing samyama on empathy, compassion,
and non-attachment, one gains union with others.

3.24

By practicing samyama on any attribute of an element
or animal—such as the strength of an elephant—
that attribute will be attained.

3.25

By practicing samyama on the inner light, one perceives
the subtle, the hidden, the mysterious and minute.

3.26

By practicing samyama on the sun,
one gains knowledge of the planetary worlds.

3.27

By practicing samyama on the moon,
one gains knowledge of the positions of stars.

3.28

By practicing samyama on the pole star,
one gains knowledge of the movement of stars.

3.29

By practicing samyama on the center point of the body,
one gains knowledge of the systems of the body.

3.30

By practicing samyama on the throat center,
one gains control over thoughts of hunger and thirst.

3.31

By practicing samyama on the "tortoise" nerve duct in the chest,
one becomes immovable.

3.32

By practicing samyama on the radiant center of the head,
one attains visions of perfected beings.

3.33

Also, all these things can be known without samyama—
in the spontaneous clear light of Realization.

3.34

By practicing samyama on the heart,
the workings of one's mind, and the minds of others,
can be known.

3.35

The bondage of experience results from a failure to discriminate   3.36
between the highest aspects of personal identity
and the true Self — which are completely different.
The spiritual aspect of personal identity is merely
an agent of Self — which is totally independent and exists
for its own sake. Practicing samyama on personal identity
as separate from Self leads to Self-knowledge.

Through this samyama there arises a spontaneous realization,   3.37
and the powers of hearing, touch, vision, taste, and smell reach
beyond the sense organs to the realm of extra-sensory intuition.

They are powers in worldly experience,   3.38
but obstacles to samadhi.

When the bonds of sense experience are loosened   3.39
and the mode of transference understood,
the consciousness of a yogi can enter another body.

By mastering the vital force that governs the upper chest,   3.40
the yogi can rise above water, swamps,
thorny paths and the like, and ascend at will.

By mastering the vital force that moves the abdomen,   3.41
the yogi can emit a blazing radiance.

Through samyama on the relationship of the ear to the Void   3.42
comes divine hearing.

Through samyama on the relationship of the body to the Void,   3.43
comes the lightness of cotton
and the ability to move through space.

Through samyama on awareness without a body —   3.44
the great incorporeal Awareness —
the veil that obscures the light dissolves.

Through samyama on the five aspects of forms —
gross manifestation, elemental nature, subtle characteristics,
interplay of the three gunas, and significance to the observer —
the yogi obtains mastery over forms.

Thus he can become the microcosm and attain all other powers,
as well as perfect the body —
which is no longer subject to laws of form.

Perfection of the body includes beauty, grace, strength,
and the crystal hardness of a diamond.

Mastery of the senses comes through samyama
on the mechanism of perception, on the essential nature
of the sense organs, on the sense of personal identity,
on the interplay of the three gunas,
and on the experience being created.

Thus the yogi can move at the speed of thought,
perceive without senses, and transmute matter
from one form to another.

Through samyama on the distinction between the spiritual
component of personal identity and the true Self,
one becomes all-knowing and attains mastery over all things.

Through indifference to all these powers, the seeds of bondage
and sorrow are destroyed and Unity is attained.

When divine beings appear to flatter and invite the yogi
to join them, attachment and pride must be avoided,
otherwise he will fall once more into ignorance.

Through samyama on the smallest moment of time and on the
succession of moments, one attains the capacity of discernment.

Thus one can distinguish between identical objects that cannot
be distinguished by species, characteristics, or position in space.

Wisdom born of discernment delivers one from ignorance.   3.55
It comprehends all things at once —
what has been and what will be —
in an eternal moment without succession.

When the mind is as clear and empty as Self,   3.56
liberation occurs and Unity obtains.

4. Liberation

Spiritual powers can be obtained by birth,
or through drugs, incantations, austerities or meditation.

4.1

The transformation of one form or level of existence to another
is the nature of the creative force.

4.2

Deeds and practices are not the direct cause of transformation,
but they can clear away obstacles,
just as the irrigator clears earth from the watercourse
so that water may flow according to its nature.

4.3

It is the sense "I am" that produces the many minds.

4.4

Though the activities of the many minds are varied,
the one Original Mind controls all.

4.5.

Of the many minds, only the mind purified by meditation
is freed from experiencing latent karma.

4.6

The karma of the yogi is neither white nor black.
The karma of others is white, black, or both.

4.7

Of the tendencies inherent in one's karma, only those for which
environmental conditions are favorable will manifest and ripen.

4.8.

Because the imprint of unmanifested tendencies transcends
birth and death, the chain of cause and effect
is unbroken by changes in form, time, and place.

4.9

Because the desire to exist is eternal, the succession of identity
images produced by these tendencies is without beginning.

4.10

These tendencies and identity images are held together
by cause and effect, grounded in desire,
and stimulated by sense experience.
When all these factors are removed,
the succession of identity images comes to an end.

4.11

The form and expression called "past"   4.12
and the form and expression called "future"
exist in the eternal Now of objects
as properties of their essential nature.

These properties are either manifest, subtle, or latent,   4.13
according to the interplay of the three gunas.

Because the three gunas comprise every form and expression   4.14
of objects, in reality there is only Unity.

Though the essential nature of an object is always the same,   4.15
its material existence is perceived differently
by individual minds according to the observer's state of being.

So if an object perceived by a single mind is no longer cognized   4.16
by that mind, can it be said to exist?

An object's existence or non-existence depends on   4.17
whether or not it is reflected in mind.

The Self, Lord of the Mind, is the immutable,   4.18
unchanging witness of the mind's fluctuations.

The mind is not self-knowing   4.19
because it can be observed as an object.

Neither can the mind be both the perceiver   4.20
and the perceived simultaneously.

To postulate an anterior mind perceiving the first,   4.21
one would have to postulate an infinite series of minds,
each perceiving the one before it,
thus causing an endless confusion of percepts and memories.

The Self is immaculate, unchangeable.   4.22
When Self is reflected in mind,
the mind abides in Self-awareness.

Self-awareness, reflecting both the knower
and the knowable, is omniscient.

4.23

Though the mind has numerous identity imprints and desires,
it is merely an agent of Self
and cannot act independently for its own sake.

4.24

One who clearly sees this distinction,
no longer confuses the mind with Self.

4.25

The mind then bends to discriminating Awareness
and is borne onwards to liberation.

4.26

Until liberation, however, distractions due to imprints and
habitual thinking may still arise when discrimination wavers.

4.27

These distractions are similar to the obstacles to Self-realization
already mentioned, and can be overcome in the same way.

4.28

One who remains undistracted even by attainment
of the highest illumination becomes —
as a result of this perfect discrimination —
what is called the "Cloud of Virtue."

4.29

Thus comes the end of illusion and freedom from karma.

4.30

All obstructions and impurities vanish,
and in the presence of infinite Awareness,
the whole of the sensory universe appears as nothing.

4.31

The interplay of the three gunas — light, inertia, vibration —
then ceases, having fulfilled its transformative purpose.

4.32

The sequence of changing moments in time
begins and ends in the eternal Now.

4.33

When the three gunas are devoid of purpose,
liberation is complete, Self is revealed as Unity,
and nothing remains to be done.

4.34

Oxherding Picture Three: Perceiving the Bull

I hear the song of the nightingale.
The sun is warm, the wind is mild,
willows are green along the shore.
Here no bull can hide!
What artist can draw that massive head,
those majestic horns?

When one hears the voice, one can sense its source.
When the six senses merge, the gate is entered.
Wherever one enters one sees the bull!
This unity is like salt in water, like color in dyestuff.
The slightest thing is not apart from Self.

Oxherding Picture Four: Catching the Bull

I seize him with a terrific struggle.
His great will and power are inexhaustible.
He charges to the high plateau far above the cloud-mists,
or in an impenetrable ravine he stands.

He dwelt in the forest a long time, but I caught him today!
Infatuation for scenery interferes with his direction.
Longing for sweeter grass, he wanders away.
His mind is still stubborn and unbridled.
If I wish him to submit, I must raise my whip.

Ashtavakra Gita

The *Ashtavakra Gita* is an ancient spiritual document of great purity and power. Pure, because it is relentlessly one-pointed. Every word is aimed at triggering Self-realization—no suggestions for self-improvement, no guidelines for moral behavior, no practical wisdom for daily life. Powerful, because repeated reading of it can be enough to send a ripe mind reeling into Truth.

Little is known about the origin of the *Ashtavakra Gita*. Ashtavakra is a name that appears in Indian lore, but almost certainly he did not write it. The author, likely an anonymous sage, merely uses the characters of Ashtavakra and King Janaka to set up a classic dialogue between guru and disciple. It's more like a guru-guru dialogue, however, because after the first salvo of wisdom from Ashtavakra, Janaka realizes the true Self, and from there it becomes difficult to distinguish between them. Because of this, some translations do away with the dialogue format and attribute everything to Ashtavakra. Indeed, since all the verses express the highest level of spoken wisdom, it would seem meaningless to attribute some to the teacher and others to the newly-enlightened disciple. Nevertheless, there is a story line.

It begins when Janaka asks Ashtavakra how to attain liberation. The sage tells him. It works! Upon hearing Ashtavakra's words Janaka realizes his True Nature. Enraptured, he describes the joy and wonder of this new state. Ashtavakra detects inconsistencies, however, and fires off a series of confrontational verses about attachment to worldly affairs. Janaka asserts that the Lord of Creation can do as he pleases. From there the dialogue intensifies and deepens until Janaka enters the final state. Dissolution.

1. Instruction on Self-Realization

Janaka said:　　　　　　　　　　　　　　　　　　　　1.1
Master, how is knowledge to be achieved,
detachment acquired, liberation attained?

Ashtavakra said:　　　　　　　　　　　　　　　　　　1.2
To be free, shun the experiences of the senses like poison.
Turn your attention to forgiveness, sincerity,
kindness, simplicity, truth.

You are not earth, water, fire, or air.　　　　　　　　1.3
Nor are you empty space.
Liberation is to know yourself as Awareness alone —
the witness of these.

Abide in Awareness with no illusion of person.　　　1.4
You will be instantly free and at peace.

You have no caste or duties.　　　　　　　　　　　　　1.5
You are invisible, unattached, formless.
You are the witness of all things. Be happy.

Right and wrong, pleasure and pain, exist in mind only.　1.6
They are not your concern.
You neither do nor enjoy. You are free.

You are the Sole Witness of all that is, forever free.　1.7
Your only bondage is not seeing This.

The thought, "I am the doer," is the bite of a poisonous snake.　1.8
To know, "I do nothing," is the wisdom of faith. Be happy.

A single understanding, "I am the One Awareness,"　1.9
consumes all suffering in the fire of an instant. Be happy.

You are unbounded Awareness — bliss, supreme bliss!　1.10
In You the universe appears,
like the mirage of a snake in a rope. Be happy.

It is true what they say, "You are what you think."
If you think you are bound you are bound.
If you think you are free you are free.

1.11

You are Self — the Solitary Witness.
You are perfect, all-pervading, One.
You are free, desireless, forever still.
The universe is but a seeming in You.

1.12

Meditate on this: "I am Awareness alone — Unity itself."
Give up the idea that you are separate, a person,
that there is within and without.

1.13

You have long been bound, thinking, "I am a person."
Let the knowledge, "I am Awareness alone,"
be the sword that frees you.

1.14

You are now and forever
free, luminous, transparent, still.
Attachment to seeking keeps one in bondage.

1.15

You are pure Awareness — the substance of the universe.
The universe exists within You.
Don't be small-minded.

1.16

You are unconditioned, changeless, formless.
You are solid, unfathomable, cool.
Desire nothing. You are Awareness.

1.17

That which has form is not real.
Only the formless is permanent.
Once this is known, you will not return to illusion.

1.18

Just as a mirror exists both within and without
the image reflected, so the supreme Self exists
both within and without the body.

1.19

Just as the same space exists both within and without a jar,
the timeless, all-pervasive One exists as Totality.

1.20

2. Joy of Self-Realization

Janaka said: 2.1
I am now spotless and at peace —
Awareness beyond consciousness!
All this time I have been duped by illusion.

By this Light alone the body and the universe appear. 2.2
I am everything, and nothing.

Seeing there is no universe or body, 2.3
by grace the Self is revealed.

As waves, foam, and bubbles are not different from water, 2.4
so the universe emanating from Self is not different from Self.

Look closely at cloth, you see only threads. 2.5
Look closely at Creation, you see only Self.

As sweetness pervades sugarcane juice, 2.6
I am the essence of Creation.

Not seeing Self, the world is materialized. 2.7
Seeing Self, the world is vanished.
A rope is not a snake, but can appear to be.

I am not other than Light. 2.8
The universe manifests at my glance.

The mirage of universe appears in me 2.9
as silver appears in mother-of-pearl,
as a snake appears in a rope,
as water appears on a desert horizon.

As a pot returns to clay, 2.10
a wave to water, a bracelet to gold,
so does the universe return to Me.

I am wonderful indeed—beyond comprehension!
I cannot decay nor ever die,
though God and all the universes
should perish to the last blade of grass.

I am wonderful indeed—beyond comprehension!
Even with a body I am One.
I neither come nor go. I am everywhere at once.

I am wonderful indeed—beyond comprehension!
I am astounded at my powers.
The universe appears within me but I do not touch it.

I am wonderful indeed—beyond comprehension!
I am everything thought or spoken, and have nothing.

In reality, knowledge, the knower,
and the capacity to know do not exist.
I am the transparent Self
in which through ignorance they appear.

Looking at One and seeing many is the cause of all misery.
The only cure is to realize that what is seen is not there.
I am One—aware, blissful, immaculate.

I am unbounded Awareness.
Only in imagination do I have limits.
Reflecting on this, I abide in the Absolute.

I am neither free nor bound.
The illusion of such things has fallen into disbelief.
Though I contain Creation, it has no substance.

Having seen for certain that this universe and body
is without form or substance,
I am revealed as Awareness alone.
Imagination has no place here.

The body exists only in imagination,
as do heaven and hell, bondage, freedom, fear.
Are these my concern? I who am pure Awareness?

2.20

I see no differences or separation.
Even the multitudes appear as a single formless desert.
To what should I cling?

2.21

I am not the body.
I do not have a body.
I am Awareness, not a person.
My thirst for life bound me to a seeming of life.

2.22

In the limitless ocean of Self
the winds of the mind roil the myriad waves of the world.

2.23

But when the wind subsides in the limitless ocean,
the ark of personhood is swallowed up —
along with the universe it carries.

2.24

And how wonderful it is!
In the limitless ocean of Self, waves of beings arise,
collide, play for a time, then disappear — as is their nature.

2.25

3. Test of Self-Realization

Ashtavakra said: 3.1
Having realized yourself as One,
being serene and indestructible,
why do you desire wealth?

Just as imagining silver in mother-of-pearl causes greed to arise,   3.2
so does ignorance of Self cause desire for illusion.

Having realized yourself as That in which   3.3
the waves of the world rise and fall,
why do you run around in turmoil?

Having realized yourself as pure Awareness,   3.4
as beautiful beyond description,
how can you remain a slave to lust?

It is strange that in a sage who has realized   3.5
Self in All and All in Self,
this sense of ownership should continue.

Strange that one abiding in the Absolute, intent on freedom,   3.6
should be vulnerable to lust and weakened
by amorous pastimes.

Strange that knowing lust as an enemy of knowledge,   3.7
one so weak and nearing death
should still crave sensual pleasure.

Strange that one who is unattached to the things   3.8
of this world and the next, who yearns for freedom,
who can discriminate between the transient and the timeless,
should yet fear the dissolution of the body.

Whether acclaimed or tormented,   3.9
the serene sage abides in Self.
He is neither gratified nor angered.

A great soul witnesses his body's actions
as if they were another's.
How can praise or blame disturb him?

3.10

Realizing the universe is illusion, having lost all curiosity,
how can one of steady mind fear death?

3.11

With whom can we compare the great soul who,
content knowing Self, remains desireless in disappointment?

3.12

Why should a person of steady mind,
who sees the nothingness of objects,
prefer one thing to another?

3.13

He who is unattached, untouched by opposites, free of desire,
experiences neither pleasure nor pain as events pass through.

3.14

4. Glorification of Self-Realization

Janaka said: 4.1
Surely one who knows Self, though he plays the game of life,
differs greatly from the world's bewildered burdened beasts.

Truly, the sage feels no elation, 4.2
though he abides in the exalted state
yearned for by Indra and all the discontented gods.

One who knows That, is not touched by virtue or vice — 4.3
just as space is not touched by smoke, though it appears to be.

Who would prevent the great soul who knows 4.4
the universe as Self, from living life as it comes?

Of the four kinds of beings, from Brahma to a blade of grass, 4.5
only the sage can renounce aversion and desire.

Rare is he who knows himself as One with no other — 4.6
the Lord of the Universe.
He acts as he knows and is never afraid.

5. Four Ways to Dissolution

Ashtavakra said: 5.1
You are immaculate, touched by nothing.
What is there to renounce?
The mind is complex—let it go.
Know the peace of dissolution.

The universe arises from you like foam from the sea. 5.2
Know yourself as One.
Enter the peace of dissolution.

Like an imagined snake in a rope, 5.3
the universe appears to exist
in the immaculate Self, but does not.
Seeing this you know, "There is nothing to dissolve."

You are perfect, changeless—through misery and happiness, 5.4
hope and despair, life and death.
This is the state of dissolution.

6. The Higher Knowledge

Janaka said:
I am infinite space. The universe is a jar.
This I know. No need to renounce, accept, or destroy.

I am a shoreless ocean. The universe makes waves.
This I know. No need to renounce, accept, or destroy.

I am mother-of–pearl. The universe is the illusion of silver.
This I know. No need to renounce, accept, or destroy.

I am in all beings. All beings are in Me.
This I know. No need to renounce, accept, or destroy.

7. Nature of Self-Realization

Janaka said:

In me, the shoreless ocean,
the ark of universe drifts here and there
on the winds of its nature.
I am not impatient.

In me, the shoreless ocean,
let the waves of the universe
rise and fall as they will.
I am neither enhanced nor diminished.

In me, the shoreless ocean,
the universe is imagined.
I am still and formless.
In this alone I abide.

The Self is not in objects,
nor are objects in the pure and infinite Self.
The Self is tranquil, free of attachment and desire.
In this alone I abide.

I am Awareness alone. The world is passing show.
How can thoughts arise of acceptance or rejection?
And where?

7.1

7.2

7.3

7.4

7.5

8. Bondage and Liberation

Ashtavakra said: 8.1
When the mind desires or grieves, accepts or rejects,
is pleased or displeased, this is bondage.

When the mind does not desire or grieve, accept or reject, 8.2
become pleased or displeased, liberation is at hand.

If the mind is attached to any experience, this is bondage. 8.3
When the mind is detached from all experience,
this is liberation.

When there is no "I" there is only liberation. 8.4
When "I" appears, bondage appears with it.
Knowing this, it is effortless to refrain
from accepting and rejecting.

9. Detachment

Ashtavakra said: 9.1
Opposing forces, duties done and left undone —
when does it end and for whom?
Considering this, be ever desireless, let go of all things,
and to the world turn an indifferent eye.

Rare and blessed is one whose desire to live, 9.2
whose desire to enjoy and to know,
has been extinguished by observing the ways of men.

Seeing all things as threefold suffering, 9.3
the sage becomes still.
Insubstantial, transient, contemptible —
the world is fit only for rejection.

Was there an age or time men existed without opposites? 9.4
Leave the opposites behind.
Be content with what is. Perfection.

The greatest seers, saints, and yogis agree on little. 9.5
Seeing this, who could not be indifferent to knowledge
and become still?

One who, through worldly indifference, 9.6
through serenity and reason,
sees his true nature and escapes illusion —
is he not a true teacher?

In the myriad forms of the universe 9.7
see the primal element alone.
You will be instantly free, and abide in Self.

Desire creates the world — renounce it! 9.8
Renounce desires and you renounce the world.
Now you may live as you are.

10. Quietude

Ashtavakra said:
Give up desire, which is the enemy.
Give up prosperity, which is born of mischief and good works.
Be indifferent.

Look upon friends, lands, wealth, houses, wives, gifts—
and all apparent good fortune—as passing show,
as a dream lasting three to five days.

Where there is desire, there is the world.
Be firm in non-attachment.
Be free of desire. Be happy.

Bondage and desire are the same.
Destroy desire and be free.
Only by detaching from the world
does one joyfully realize Self.

You are One—Awareness itself.
The universe is not aware, nor is anything in it.
In reality it does not exist.
Even ignorance is unreal. What is left to know?

Attached as you have been to kingdoms,
sons, wives, bodies, pleasures—life after life—
still they are now lost forever.

Prosperity, pleasure, pious deeds… Enough!
In the dreary forest of the world the mind finds no rest.

For how many lifetimes have you done hard and painful labor
with body, mind, and speech? It is time to stop.

11. Wisdom

Ashtavakra said: 11.1
Existence, non-existence, change — this is the nature of things.
Realizing this, stillness, serenity and bliss naturally follow.

One who knows for certain that 11.2
"Self creates All and is alone,"
becomes still, desireless, unattached.

One who knows for certain that adversity and success 11.3
come and go in obedience to destiny, finds contentment.
He neither desires nor grieves.

One who knows for certain that birth and death, 11.4
happiness and misery, come and go in obedience to destiny,
sees nothing to accomplish.
He engages in non-action, and in action remains unattached.

One who has realized that only by caring is misery caused 11.5
in the world, becomes free, happy, serene, desireless.

"I am not the body, nor is the body my possession — 11.6
I am Awareness itself."
One who realizes this for certain
has no memory of things done or left undone.
There is only the Absolute.

"From Brahma to the last blade of grass, I alone exist." 11.7
One who knows this for certain is immaculate,
serene, unconflicted. Attainment has no meaning.

One who knows for certain that this manifold, wonderful 11.8
universe is Void, becomes desireless Awareness,
and abides in the stillness of No-thing.

12. Abiding in the Self

Janaka said:
Becoming first intolerant of action, then of excessive speech,
then of thought itself, I come to be Here.

Neither sounds nor other sense perceptions attract my attention.
Even the Self is unperceived.
The mind is free, undistracted, one-pointed.
And I am Here.

Effort is required to concentrate a distracted mind
superimposed with illusion.
Seeing this, I remain Here.

Nothing to reject, nothing to accept.
No joy, no sorrow. I am forever Here.

The four stages of life, life without stages,
meditation, renunciation, objects of mind —
nothing but distractions. I am content to be Here.

Doing and not-doing both arise from ignorance.
I choose to remain Here.

Thinking of the unthinkable One unavoidably conjures thought.
I choose no-thought and delight in Here.

Blessed is he who attains this by effort.
Blessed is he who is such by nature.

13. Happiness

Janaka said: 13.1
The tranquil state of knowing Self is rare—
even among those who own but a loincloth.
I therefore neither renounce nor accept and am happy.

The body is strained by practices.   13.2
The tongue tires of scripture.
The mind numbs with meditation.
Detached from all this, I live as I am.

Realizing that nothing is done, I do what comes and am happy.   13.3

Yogis who preach either effort or non-effort   13.4
are still attached to the body.
I neither agree nor disagree with any of that, and am happy.

I have nothing to gain or lose by standing,   13.5
walking, or sitting down.
So whether I stand, walk, or sit, I am happy.

I do not lose by sleeping or attain by effort.   13.6
Not thinking in terms of loss or gain, I am happy.

Pleasure and pain fluctuate and are inconsistent.   13.7
Without good or bad, I live happily.

14. Tranquility

Janaka said:
Though appearing asleep like other men,
one whose interest in the world is exhausted —
whose mind has been emptied,
who thinks only by inadvertence — is in reality, Awake.

When desire has melted, how can there be wealth or friends,
or the seduction of senses?
Of what use is scripture and knowledge?

I have realized the supreme Self, Awareness, the One.
I am indifferent to bondage and freedom.
I have no need for liberation.

The inner condition of one who is devoid of doubt
yet moves among creatures of illusion,
can only be known by those like him.

15. Knowledge of the Self

Ashtavakra said: 15.1
A man of open intuition may realize Self upon hearing
a casual instruction, while a man of cluttered intellect
inquires bewildered for a lifetime.

Indifference to the world's offerings is liberation.   15.2
Attraction to the world's offerings is the suffering of bondage.
This is the truth. Now do as you please.

This knowledge of Truth   15.3
turns an eloquent, wise, and active man,
mute, empty, and inert.
Lovers of the world therefore shun it.

You are not the body.   15.4
You do not have a body.
You neither do nor enjoy.
You are Awareness alone — the timeless Witness.
You are free. Go in happiness.

Attachment and aversion are attributes of the mind.   15.5
You are not the mind. You are consciousness itself —
changeless, undivided, free. Go in happiness.

Realize Self in All and All in Self.   15.6
Be free of personal identity and the sense of "mine."
Be happy.

You are That in which the universe appears   15.7
like waves appearing in the ocean.
You are Awareness itself. No need to worry.

Have faith, my son, have faith.   15.8
You are Awareness alone, the Self, the One.
You are the Lord of Nature.

The body is made of worldly stuff.   15.9
It comes, it lingers, it goes.
The Self neither comes nor goes, but is forever Here.
Why mourn the body?

If the body lasts until the end of time or perishes today,   15.10
is there gain or loss for you? You who are pure Awareness?

Let the waves of universe rise and fall as they will.   15.11
You have nothing to gain or lose. You are the ocean.

You are the substance of Creation.   15.12
The universe is You.
Who is it that thinks he can accept or reject it?
And where does he stand?

In You, who is One — immaculate, pure Awareness —   15.13
how does birth, action, or a separate person arise?

Whatever you perceive is You and You alone.   15.14
How can bracelets, armlets, and anklets
be other than the gold they are made of?

Leave behind such distinctions as, "I am he,"   15.15
and, "I am not this." Consider everything Self.
Be desireless and be happy.

Ignorance creates the universe.   15.16
In reality, One alone exists.
There is no person or god other than You.

One who knows for certain that the universe is illusion,   15.17
a seeming, becomes desireless pure Awareness,
and finds peace in the realm of No-thing.

In the ocean of existence only One is, was, and ever will be.   15.18
You are neither bound nor free.
Live content and be happy.

Do not stir the mind with "yes" or "no."
You are pure Awareness.
Be still, and abide in the bliss of Self.

15.19

Give up completely all contemplation.
Hold nothing in the mind or heart.
You are the Self, forever free.
Of what use is thinking to you?

15.20

16. Special Instruction

Ashtavakra said:　　　　　　　　　　　　　　　　　　　16.1
You can recite and discuss scripture all you want,
but until you drop everything you will never know Truth.

You can enjoy and work and meditate,　　　　　　　　　16.2
but you will still yearn for That which is beyond all experience,
and in which all desires are extinguished.

Everyone is miserable because they exert constant effort,　16.3
but no one understands this.
A ripe mind can become unshackled
upon hearing this one instruction.

The master idler, to whom even blinking is a bother,　　16.4
is happy. But he is the only one.

When the mind is free of opposites like,　　　　　　　16.5
"This is done," and, "This is yet undone,"
one becomes indifferent to merit, wealth,
pleasure and liberation.

One who abhors sense objects avoids them.　　　　　　16.6
One who desires them becomes ensnared.
One who neither abhors nor desires
is neither detached nor attached.

As long as there is desire —　　　　　　　　　　　　16.7
which is the absence of discrimination —
there will be attachment and non-attachment.
This is the cause of the world.

Indulgence creates attachment.　　　　　　　　　　　16.8
Aversion creates abstinence.
Like a child, the sage is free of both
and thus lives on as a child.

One who is attached to the world   16.9
thinks renouncing it will relieve his misery.
One who is attached to nothing is free,
and does not feel miserable even in the world.

He who claims liberation as his own,   16.10
as an attainment of a person,
is neither enlightened nor a seeker.
He suffers his own misery.

Though Hara, Hari,   16.11
or the lotus-born Brahma himself instruct you,
until you know Nothing, you will never know Self.

17. The True Knower

Ashtavakra said:　17.1
One has attained knowledge and reaped the fruits of yoga
who is content, purified of attachments,
and at home in solitude.

The knower of Truth is never miserable in the world,　17.2
for the whole universe is filled with Himself alone.

As the foliage of the *neem* tree does not please　17.3
an elephant who delights in *sallaki* leaves,
so do sense objects not please one who delights in Self.

Rare in the world is one who does not relish past enjoyments,　17.4
nor yearn for enjoyments to come.

Those who desire pleasure and those who desire liberation　17.5
are both common in the world. Rare is the great soul
who desires neither enjoyment nor liberation.

Rare is the right-minded person　17.6
who neither covets nor shuns
religion, wealth, pleasure, life or death.

The sage neither cares for the universe　17.7
nor desires its dissolution.
He lives happily with whatever comes his way.
He is blessed.

Knowing Self, mind empty and at peace,　17.8
the sage lives happily —
seeing, hearing, touching, smelling, eating...

There is no attachment or non-attachment　17.9
for one in whom the ocean of the world has dried up.
His look is vacant, senses still.
His actions have no purpose.

The sage is neither asleep nor awake.   17.10
His eyes are neither open or closed.
Thus, for the liberated soul, everywhere there is only This.

The liberated soul abides in Self alone and is pure of heart.   17.11
He lives always and everywhere, free of desire.

Seeing, hearing, touching, smelling, eating,   17.12
taking, speaking, walking, the great soul
exerts neither effort nor non-effort. He is truly free.

The liberated soul does not blame or praise,   17.13
give or take, rejoice or become angry.
He is everywhere unattached and free.

The great soul remains poised and undisturbed,   17.14
whether in the presence of a passionate woman,
or observing the approach of his death. He is truly free.

The sage sees no difference between happiness and misery,   17.15
man and woman, adversity and success.
Everything is seen to be the same.

In the sage there is neither violence nor mercy,   17.16
arrogance nor humility, anxiety nor wonder.
His worldly life is exhausted.
He has transcended his role as a person.

The liberated one neither avoids experience nor craves it.   17.17
He enjoys what comes, and what does not.

The sage is not conflicted by states of stillness and thought.   17.18
His mind is empty. His home is the Absolute.

Though he may perform actions, the sage does not act.   17.19
Desires extinguished, free of thoughts of "I" and "mine,"
he knows with absolute certainty that nothing exists.

The sage is free. His empty mind no longer projects
delusion, dreaming, dullness.
This state is indescribable.

18. Peace

Ashtavakra said: 18.1
Praise That, which is bliss itself,
which is by nature stillness and light,
and which by its knowing reveals the world as a dream.

One may enjoy the abundant pleasures of the world,   18.2
but will never be happy until giving them up.

How can one whose innermost heart has been scorched   18.3
by the sun of sorrow that comes from duty,
be happy until the sweet rain of torrential stillness?

The universe is but a thought in consciousness.   18.4
In Reality it is nothing.
One who sees the true nature of existence and non-existence
never ceases to exist.

The Self, which is absolute, effortless, timeless, immaculate,   18.5
is without limits and at no distance from you.
You are forever It.

For those whose vision becomes unclouded,   18.6
illusion evaporates and Self becomes known.
All sorrow is instantly dispelled.

Seeing everything is imagination,   18.7
knowing the Self as timelessly free,
the sage lives as a child.

Knowing himself as Absolute,   18.8
knowing existence and non-existence to be imagination only,
what is there for the desireless one to learn, say, or do?

Knowing for certain that all is Self,   18.9
the sage has no trace of thoughts
such as, "I am this" or, "I am not that."

The yogi who finds stillness is neither distracted nor focused.   18.10
He knows neither pleasure nor pain.
Ignorance dispelled, he is free of knowing.

Heaven or poverty, gain or loss, society or solitude…   18.11
to the yogi free of conditioning there is no difference.

Religious merit, sensory pleasure, worldly prosperity,   18.12
discrimination between this and that—
these have no significance to the yogi free of opposites,
such as, "I do this" and, "This I do not."

The yogi who is liberated while living   18.13
has no duties in this world,
no attachments in his heart.
His life proceeds without him.

For the great soul who abides beyond desire,   18.14
where is illusion? Where is the universe?
Where is meditation on That?
Where even is liberation from them?

He who sees the world may try to renounce it.   18.15
But what can the desireless one do?
He sees there is nothing to see.

He who has seen the supreme Brahma thinks, "I am Brahma."   18.16
But he who has transcended all thought, what can he think?
He knows no other than Self.

He achieves self-control who sees his own distraction.   18.17
But the great soul is not distracted.
He has nothing to achieve.
He has nothing to do.

The sage may live as an ordinary man, but he is not.   18.18
He sees he is neither focused nor distracted,
and finds no fault with himself.

He who is beyond existence and non-existence —
who is wise, satisfied, and free of desire —
does nothing, though the world may see him in motion.

18.19

The wise one is not troubled by action or inactivity.
He lives happily, doing whatever gets done.

18.20

Like a leaf in the wind,
the liberated one is untethered from life —
desireless, independent, free.

18.21

For one who has transcended the world
there is no joy or sorrow.
Mind stilled, the body lives on without him.

18.22

One who knows Self, whose mind is serene and spotless,
does not desire to give up anything,
nor does he miss what is not there.

18.23

His mind being in a natural state of emptiness,
the wise one knows nothing of honor and dishonor.
He does what comes to be done.

18.24

One who acts knowing,
"This is done by the body, not by Me, the Self,"
indeed does nothing, no matter how much acting takes place.

18.25

The liberated one acts without claiming to be acting,
but he is no fool.
He is blessed and happy, even though in the world.

18.26

Having had enough of the endless workings of the mind,
the wise one comes to rest.
He neither thinks, nor knows, nor hears, nor sees.

18.27

Beyond stillness, beyond distraction, the great soul
thinks nothing of liberation or bondage.
Having seen the universe is Void —
even though it seems to exist — he is God.

18.28

He who believes he is a person is constantly acting,
even when the body is at rest.
The sage knows he is not a person and therefore does nothing,
even when the body is in motion.

18.29

The mind of the liberated one is neither troubled nor pleased.
It is actionless, motionless, desireless, and free of doubt.

18.30

The liberated one does not exert effort to meditate or act.
Action and meditation just happen.

18.31

Hearing ultimate Truth, the dull-witted man is bewildered.
The wise man hearing Truth
retreats within and appears dull-witted.

18.32

The ignorant practice meditation and no-thought.
The wise, like men in deep sleep, do nothing.

18.33

The ignorant man finds no peace either by effort or non-effort.
The wise man by Truth alone is stilled.

18.34

Though they are by nature Self alone,
pure intelligence, love and perfection —
though they transcend the universe and are clearness itself —
men of the world will not see this
through meditation and practices.

18.35

The ignorant man will never be liberated
by his repetitious practices.
Blessed is he who, by simple understanding,
enters timeless freedom.

18.36

Because he desires to know God,
the ignorant man can never become That.
The wise man *is* God because he is free of desire
and knows nothing.

18.37

Unable to stand steady, and eager for salvation,
the ignorant perpetuate the illusion of world.
Seeing the world as the source of all misery,
the wise cut it off at the root.

18.38

The fool thinks peace comes by controlling the mind.
He will never attain it.
The wise one knows Truth, and is stillness itself.

18.39

For he who thinks knowledge is things and ideas,
how can there be Self-knowledge?
The wise do not see separate things, only the timeless Self.

18.40

The fool tries to control the mind with the mind — what folly!
The wise one delights in Self alone.
There is no mind to master.

18.41

Some believe in existence.
Others believe nothing exists.
Rare is the one who believes nothing and is never confused.

18.42

Weak intellectuals may believe the Self is One without other.
But being mired in illusion they do not actually know Self,
so live out their lives in misery.

18.43

The mind of one seeking liberation
depends on things for perception.
The mind of the liberated one perceives no-thing
and is free of desire.

18.44

Timid men fear sensory experience much as they do tigers.
They seek refuge in caves and try to un-think the world.

18.45

Sensory experiences are like elephants who,
upon encountering a desireless man, see him as a lion.
They immediately turn on their heels,
or if unable to escape, stay on to flatter and serve him.

18.46

A man with no doubts, who knows Self,
has no need of practice or liberation.
Seeing, hearing, touching, smelling, eating,
he lives happily as he is.

18.47

One whose mind is emptied and unconflicted
by the mere hearing of Truth,
sees nothing to do, nothing to avoid,
nothing to warrant his indifference.

18.48

The sage does whatever appears to be done,
without thinking of good or bad.
His actions are those of a child.

18.49

Depending on nothing, one finds happiness.
Depending on nothing, one attains the Absolute.
Depending on nothing, one passes through tranquility
to One Self.

18.50

When one realizes he is neither the actor
nor the one who watches, the mind-storm is stilled.

18.51

The actions of the sage, free of pretense and motive,
shine like clear light.
Not so those of the deluded seeker, who affects
a peaceful demeanor while remaining firmly attached.

18.52

Unbounded, unfettered,
untethered from the projections of mind,
the wise are free to play and enjoy,
or retire to mountain caves.

18.53

Whether honoring a spiritual scholar, a god, or holy shrine,
whether seeing a desirable woman, a king, or beloved friend,
the heart of the sage is unmoved.

18.54

Though his servants, sons, wives, daughters, grandchildren,
and all his relatives ridicule and despise him,
the sage is undismayed.

18.55

Though pleased he is not pleasured.   18.56
Though pained he does not suffer.
This wonderful state is understood only by those like him.

The belief in duty creates a relative world for its performance.   18.57
The wise one knows Himself to be formless,
timeless, all-pervasive, immaculate,
and thus transcends duty and world.

Even doing nothing, the dull one is anxious and distracted.   18.58
Even amidst great action, the wise one remains still.

Even in practical life the wise one remains happy.   18.59
Happy to sit, happy to sleep, happy to move about,
happy to speak, happy to eat…

Because he knows Self,   18.60
the wise one is not disrupted by practical life.
He is deep and still, like a vast lake.
He is not like ordinary people.
His sorrows have vanished.

For the deluded, even rest is an activity.   18.61
For the wise, even action bears the fruit of stillness.

The deluded are often adverse to the things of life.   18.62
To one with no thought for body,
attachment and aversion have no meaning.

The deluded mind is caught up in thinking and not thinking.   18.63
Though the mind of the wise one
may think what thoughts come, he is not aware of it.

The sage sees nothing being done,   18.64
even when performed by his hands.
Like a child he is pure, and acts without reason.

Blessed indeed is he who knows Self.
Though seeing, hearing, touching, smelling, eating,
he never desires nor changes.

18.65

For one who is void and changeless,
where is the world and its imaginings?
Where is the end? Where is the possibility of it?

18.66

Glorious indeed is he who, free of desire,
embodies bliss itself. He has become absorbed in Self.

18.67

In short, the great soul who has realized Truth
is free of desire, enjoyment, and liberation.
In all of space and time, he is attached to nothing.

18.68

What remains for one who is Awareness itself,
who sees the non-existence of a phenomenal world
created by the mere thought of a name?

18.69

Peace is natural for one who knows for certain nothing exists,
who sees appearances are illusion,
and to whom the inexpressible is apparent.

18.70

Rules of conduct, detachment, renunciation, asceticism—
what are these to one who sees the unreality of things,
to one who is the Light of Awareness?

18.71

How can there be joy or sorrow, bondage or liberation,
for one who perceives non-existence and lights the infinite?

18.72

Until Self-realization, illusion prevails.
But the sage lives without thoughts of "I" or "mine."
His tether to illusion is severed.

18.73

What is knowledge? What is universe?
What are thoughts like, "I am the body,"
or "The body is mine"?
The sage is imperishable and sorrowless.
He is Self alone.

18.74

When a weak man gives up meditation,
he falls prey to whims and desires.

18.75

Even hearing Truth, the man of dull intellect
holds on to illusion. Through effort and suppression
he may appear outwardly composed,
but inside he craves the world.

18.76

Though others may see him working, the sage does nothing.
Awakening has banished effort.
He finds no reason to do or say.

18.77

The sage is fearless, unassailable.
No darkness, no light, nothing to lose.
Nothing.

18.78

Patience, discrimination, even fearlessness —
what use are these to the sage?
His nature cannot be described.
He is not a person.

18.79

No heaven, no hell, no liberation for the living.
In short, consciousness is void. What more can be said?

18.80

The sage neither yearns for fulfillment
nor frets over non-attainment.
His mind is cool and brimming with sweetness.

18.81

Detached from desire, the sage neither praises peace
nor blames the wicked. Equally content
in happiness and misery, he would not change a thing.

18.82

The sage neither rejects the world nor desires Self.
He is free of joy and sorrow.
He does not live and cannot die.

18.83

The wise one lives without hope.
He has no attachment to his children, wife, or anyone.
Pleasure means nothing to him. His life is glorious.

18.84

The sage wanders about as he pleases   18.85
and lives on whatever may come.
Contentment ever dwells in his heart.
And when the sun sets, he rests where he is.

Rooted in being, no thought of being born or reborn,   18.86
the great soul is indifferent to the death or birth of his body.

The wise one stands alone,   18.87
caring for nothing, bereft of possessions.
He goes where he will, unhindered by opposites,
his doubts rent asunder. He is truly blessed.

The wise one has no sense of "mine."   18.88
To him, earth, stone, and gold are the same.
The knots of his heart have unraveled.
He knows neither ignorance nor sorrow.
He is excellent in every way.

The liberated soul has no desire in his heart.   18.89
He is content and indifferent. He has no equal.

Only one free of desire knows nothing of knowing,   18.90
says nothing needs saying, sees nothing to see.

He who is without desire excels, be he beggar or king.   18.91
He no longer sees good or bad.

What is lust or restraint or the desire for Truth   18.92
to the yogi who has reached life's goal,
who embodies sincerity and virtue?

The inner experience of one who is free of desire and suffering,   18.93
who is content and reposes in Self—
how can it be described, and of whom?

The wise one's state never varies. 18.94
Sleeping soundly, he is not asleep.
Lying in reverie, he is not dreaming.
Eyes open, he is not wakeful.

The great soul seems to think, but has no thoughts. 18.95
He seems to have sense perceptions, but does not experience.
He seems to have intelligence, but is empty-minded.
He appears to be a person, but is not.

The sage is neither happy nor miserable, 18.96
neither detached nor attached,
neither liberated nor seeking liberation.
He is neither this nor that.

Even while distracted, the blessed one is still. 18.97
In meditation, he does not meditate.
In ignorance, he remains clear.
Though learned, he knows nothing.

The liberated one—who abides unconditionally in Self, 18.98
who is free of the concept of action and duty,
who is always and everywhere the same—is desireless.
He does not worry about what he did or did not do.

The wise one is neither pleased by praise 18.99
nor annoyed by blame.
He neither rejoices in life nor fears death.

One of tranquil mind seeks neither crowds nor wilderness. 18.100
He is the same wherever he goes.

19. Repose in the Self

Janaka said: 19.1
With the tongs of Truth I have plucked the thorn of thinking
from the innermost cave of my heart.

Where is meditation, pleasure, prosperity, discrimination?   19.2
Where is duality? Where even is Unity?
I abide in the glory of Self.

Where is past and future, or even present?   19.3
Where is space, or even eternity?
I abide in the glory of Self.

Where is God? Where is not-God?   19.4
Where is good and evil, confusion and clarity?
I abide in the glory of Self.

Where is sleeping, dreaming, waking, or even the fourth state?   19.5
Where is fear? I abide in the glory of Self.

Where is close or far, in or out, gross or subtle?   19.6
I abide in the glory of Self.

Where is life and death?   19.7
Where is the world and worldly relations?
Where is distraction and stillness?
I abide in the glory of Self.

There is no need to talk about the three ends of life.   19.8
Talk of yoga is without purpose.
Even talking about Truth is irrelevant.
I rest in Self alone.

20. Liberation-in-Life

Janaka said: 20.1
Where are the elements, the body, the organs, the mind?
Where is the Void? Where is despair?
My nature is transparent clearness.

Where is scripture?   20.2
Where is self-knowledge?
Where is no-mind?
Where is contentment and freedom from desire?
I am empty of two-ness.

Where is knowledge and ignorance?   20.3
Where is "I"? Where is "this"? Where is "mine"?
Where is bondage and liberation?
Self has no attributes.

Where is the unfolding of karma?   20.4
Where is liberation in life? Or even liberation at death?
There is only One.

Where is the doer or enjoyer?   20.5
Where is the origin or end of thought?
Where is direct or reflected knowledge?
There is no person here.

Where is the world?   20.6
Where is the seeker of liberation?
Where is the contemplative?
Where is the man of knowledge?
Where is the soul in bondage?
Where is the liberated soul?
My nature is Unity.

Where are creation and destruction?   20.7
Where is the end and the means?
Where is the seeker? Where is attainment?
I am One.

Where is the knower? Where is knowing?
Where is the known, or knowledge itself?
Where is anything? Where is nothing?
I am pure Awareness.

20.8

Where is distraction, concentration, knowledge, or delusion?
Where is joy or sorrow? I am stillness.

20.9

Where is the relative? Where the transcendent?
Where is happiness or misery? I am empty of thought.

20.10

Where is illusion? Where is existence?
Where is attachment or non-attachment?
Where is person? Where is God?
I am Awareness.

20.11

Where is activity or inactivity?
Where is liberation or bondage?
I am timeless, indivisible.
I am Self alone.

20.12

Where are principles and scriptures?
Where is the disciple or teacher?
Where is the reason for life?
I am the boundless Absolute.

20.13

Where is existence or non-existence?
Where is Unity or duality?
No-thing emanates from me.
No more can be said.

20.14

Oxherding Picture Five: Taming the Bull

The whip and rope are necessary,
else he might stray off down some dusty road.
Being well trained, he becomes naturally gentle.
Then, unfettered, he obeys his master.

When one thought arises, another thought follows.
When the first thought springs from enlightenment,
all subsequent thoughts are true.
Through delusion, one makes everything untrue.
Delusion is the result of subjectivity.
Hold the nose-ring tight and do not allow even a doubt.

Oxherding Picture Six: Riding the Bull Home

Mounting the bull, slowly I return homeward.
The voice of my flute intones through the evening.
Measuring with hand-beats the pulsating harmony,
I direct the endless rhythm.
Whoever hears this melody will join me.

This struggle is over. Gain and loss are assimilated.
I sing the song of the village woodsman,
and play the tunes of the children.
Astride the bull, I observe the clouds overhead.
Onward I go, no matter who may try to call me back.

Dhammapada
Sayings of Gotama Buddha

The man who came to be known as Buddha (an honorific meaning "Enlightened One" or "Awakened One") was born in the sixth century B.C., heir to a small kingdom in the Himalayan foothills of what is now Nepal. His name was Siddhartha Gotama. At the age of twenty-nine he experienced a deeply disturbing epiphany about suffering and death that led him to abandon his life of luxury and seek an ultimate answer in the forest. After six years of meditation and austerities, however, he realized he was no closer to Truth than when he'd begun. In desperation he sat beneath the now famous Bodhi tree and vowed not to get up until he was enlightened. It happened. Afterwards, he stood and walked a few steps from where he'd sat. He looked back and shook his head. He sat again in the spot beneath the tree and said, "This cannot be taught."

For the next forty-five years, however, he traveled throughout northern India expounding the *Dhamma*—the Teaching, the Way. A large order of monks and nuns formed around him and hundreds or even thousands might gather for one of his talks. At the age of eighty he died peacefully in the town of Kusinara, surrounded by disciples.

The *Dhammapada* ("aspects of the *Dhamma*") is widely regarded as the most succinct expression of Buddha's teaching found in the Pali Canon. In Theravedic Buddhist countries it is used in monasteries as a primer for novices, and by the general population as an essential guidebook for resolving the problems of daily life. It contains profound instructions for seekers of spiritual enlightenment, as well as basic principles for living a moral life free of suffering.

1. Opposite Ways

The experience of life is created by mind.   1.1
Thought precedes experience.
If one speaks and acts with a clouded mind,
suffering follows, as the wheel of the ox-cart follows the ox.

The experience of life is created by mind.   1.2
Thought precedes experience.
If one speaks and acts with a clear mind,
contentment follows like a faithful shadow.

"He insulted me! He attacked me!   1.3
He cheated me! He robbed me!"
One who holds these thoughts will never be free of hate.

"He insulted me! He attacked me!   1.4
He cheated me! He robbed me!"
One who is free of these thoughts will be free of hate.

Hatred in this world is not ended by hating.   1.5
Hatred is ended by not hating.
This truth has no exceptions.

Most people forget they will soon be dead.   1.6
Those who remember put an end to their quarrels.

One who lives for pleasure, senses unchecked,   1.7
who eats too much, works too little, and lacks vital energy,
is bent to the intent of Mara the Beguiler,
just as a weak tree is bent by wind.

One who is unmoved by pleasure, senses restrained,   1.8
who eats in moderation, works diligently,
and retains vital energy, is not beguiled by Mara,
just as a rock is not ruffled by wind.

One who would wear the saffron robe who is clouded,
lacking in virtue and ignorant of truth,
is not worthy of the saffron robe.

1.9

One who would wear the saffron robe who is clear,
well established in virtue and truth,
is worthy of the saffron robe.

1.10

One who takes the unreal to be real
will never see the real,
being beguiled by the unreal.

1.11

One who knows the unreal is not real
will come to see the real,
being no longer beguiled by the unreal.

1.12

Desire permeates a clouded mind
as rain permeates a badly thatched house.

1.13

Desire does not permeate a clear mind,
as rain does not permeate a well-thatched house.

1.14

Selfish action brings grief.
Grief now, grief hereafter, grief in both.
Seeing the selfishness of one's actions, one forever grieves.

1.15

Selfless action brings joy.
Joy now, joy hereafter, joy in both.
Seeing the selflessness of one's actions, one is free of grief.

1.16

He who does evil suffers. Suffers now, suffers hereafter.
In both he knows, "I have done evil."
He burns in torment at the thought of his evil,
and is born to a realm of suffering.

1.17

He who does good is content. Content now, content hereafter.
In both he knows, "I have done good."
He rejoices in the thought of his goodness,
and exists in a state of contentment.

1.18

One who recites many religious teachings
but is careless about putting them into practice,
is like a cowherd counting cows that are not his.
He cannot taste the milk of spiritual life.

1.19

One who recites few religious teachings
but is faithful to Dhamma,
who has overcome desire, hatred and delusion,
whose mind is clear, who clings to nothing now or hereafter,
indeed lives the life of spirit.

1.20

2. Awareness

Awareness is the domain of no-death.
Delusion is the domain of death.
One who is Aware will never die.
One who is deluded never lives.

The wise — knowing Awareness, rejoicing in Awareness —
abide with delight in the domain of the great.

The wise — earnest in meditation,
self-remembered, absorbed in Awareness —
realize boundless Nirvana, and secure the peace of freedom.

Glory grows for one who is energetic, self-remembered,
considerate, restrained, selfless, mindful,
and who lives Dhamma.

The wise, through energy and mindfulness,
earnestness and restraint,
become an island no flood can submerge.

The foolish abandon themselves to delusion.
The wise treasure only Awareness.

Do not succumb to delusion.
Do not devote your energy to desire.
Aware and self-remembered,
the wise are content and fulfilled.

The sage, his ignorance dissolved in Awareness,
abides sorrowless at the summit of insight,
and looks upon the deluded, sorrowing masses
as one gazing from a mountaintop on the valley below.

Aware among the deluded, awake among the sleeping,
the sage moves effortlessly to the fore,
like a racehorse running with nags.

With Awareness, Indra became supreme among gods.   2.10
Awareness is ever revered. Delusion is ever rejected.

The seeker who reveres Awareness and rejects delusion   2.11
becomes like a fire, burning through the fetters of his bondage.

The seeker who reveres Awareness and rejects delusion   2.12
cannot fail. Nirvana is ever near.

3. Mind

Mind is erratic, restless, difficult to observe, difficult to control.
The sage sets it straight, as the fletcher sets straight an arrow.

3.1

Like a fish taken from water and thrown on the ground,
the mind twists and struggles in Mara's domain of death.

3.2

Mind is capricious, flitting where it pleases, difficult to tame.
It is good to tame the mind. The tamed mind becomes content.

3.3

Mind is ephemeral, appearing where it pleases,
difficult to observe. It is good to observe the mind.
The observed mind becomes still.

3.4

Mind is intangible.
Alone, wandering far, it haunts the cave of the heart.
One who masters the mind breaks the bonds of Mara.

3.5

One whose mind is unruly, who does not know Dhamma,
who waivers in faith, will not be fulfilled.

3.6

He has no fear whose mind is still, who is free of desire,
who sees through the illusion of good and evil.
He is Awake.

3.7

Seeing the body is fragile as a vase,
fortify the citadel of the mind.
Engage Mara with Awareness.
Guard what you gather without being attached.

3.8

Alas, soon enough, this body will lie on the ground.
Cast off, lifeless, devoid of consciousness,
useless as a piece of rotten wood.

3.9

Whatever an enemy may do to an enemy,
or one man of hate do to another,
far greater harm is done to oneself
by the ignorance of one's own mind.

3.10

Whatever a father or mother or any other relative
can give to a child, far greater good is bestowed on oneself
by the clarity of one's own mind.

4. Flowers

Who shall master the earth and gods,
and conquer the death-realm of Yama?
Who chooses Dhamma as an expert chooses a flower?

4.1

The earnest seeker shall master the earth and gods,
and conquer the death-realm of Yama.
The earnest seeker chooses Dhamma,
as an expert chooses a flower.

4.2

Knowing the body to be as insubstantial as foam,
seeing it has no more substance than a mirage,
one breaks the flower-tipped arrows of Mara
and becomes invisible to the Lord of Death.

4.3

One absorbed in plucking the sense-flowers of Mara
is surprised by death and swept suddenly away,
like a sleeping village in the path of a great flood.

4.4

One obsessed with plucking the sense-flowers of Mara
is never satisfied, and all too soon drowns in death.

4.5

The sage wanders through life as the bee wanders
from flower to flower. Nectar is taken,
but the beauty and fragrance of the blossom is untouched.

4.6

Do not concern yourself with the faults of others,
with what they have done or not done.
Think only of what you have done and have yet to do.

4.7

Elegant words, spoken but not lived,
are beautiful flowers with no fragrance or promise of fruit.

4.8

Elegant words, lived as they are spoken,
are beautiful fragrant flowers destined to bear fruit.

4.9

Just as many garlands can be fashioned from a heap of flowers,
so a man can fashion many good things from his life.

4.10

The fragrance of flowers does not travel against the wind.   4.11
Nor does the perfume of sandalwood, rosebay or jasmine.
Yet the scent of a virtuous life does travel against the wind.
It imbues the far reaches of everywhere.

The perfumes of sandalwood, crepe jasmine, blue lotus,   4.12
flowering jasmine — none surpass the fragrance of virtue.

The fragrances of sandalwood and jasmine are barely detectable   4.13
compared to the perfume of a virtuous life.
It permeates even the realm of the gods.

Those who abound in virtue, who live in Awareness,   4.14
who realize the Real,
are invisible to Mara the Beguiler.

Just as a beautiful, fragrant lotus blooms   4.15
in a pile of garbage beside the road,
so does a follower of the Way of Buddha,   4.16
blossom in a world of blind ignorance.

5. The Deluded

One night is long to the wakeful.   5.1
Seven miles is far for the weary.
To the deluded ones who do not know Dhamma,
the cycle of birth and death is endless.

If while walking the path you fail to meet your equal or better,   5.2
steadfastly make your way alone.
The deluded are not fit companions.

The deluded one worries, thinking,   5.3
"I have sons. I have wealth."
He has not even himself, much less sons or wealth.

The deluded one who knows he is deluded   5.4
is to that extent clear.
The deluded one who thinks he sees clearly is truly deluded.

A deluded man may associate with an Awakened One   5.5
his whole life, yet remain unaware of Dhamma.
Much as the spoon cannot taste soup.

A mindful man, however, may only briefly encounter   5.6
an Awakened One, yet instantly know Dhamma.
Much as the tongue immediately tastes soup.

The deluded one, unaware of his delusion,   5.7
is an enemy unto himself.
Committing ignorant deeds, he reaps bitter fruit.

Deeds done in ignorance bring regret.   5.8
Suffering and repentance are extracted.
Weeping covers the face with tears.

Deeds done in Awareness bring no regret.   5.9
Joy and happiness well up, and are gladly received.

The deluded one thinks evil tastes sweet   5.10
until the consequences ripen.
When the consequences ripen, there is only misery.

A deluded ascetic may measure his food   5.11
with the tip of a blade of grass, month after month,
yet he is not worth a sixteenth part
of one who knows Dhamma.

Like fresh milk, an evil deed does not immediately sour.   5.12
It follows the deluded one,
smoldering like coals covered with ashes,
until it is ready to burn.

For the deluded one, even spiritual knowledge is harmful.   5.13
It goes to his head and causes imbalance.

The deluded aspirant desires unwarranted honors,   5.14
preeminence among his fellows, authority in the monastery,
homage from surrounding households.

"Let both householder and monk believe that I,   5.15
my personal self, have achieved great wisdom.
Let them come to me for guidance in all things."
This is the intention of the deluded aspirant—
to feed desire and pride.

One road leads to earthly delights,   5.16
another leads to Nirvana.
Let the observer of the Way of Buddha
delight not in honors, but in solitude.

6. The Sage

Look upon the man who tells you your faults
as a revealer of hidden treasure. Associate with the sage
who sees clearly and speaks reprovingly.
Only good can come of this.

6.1

The sage counsels, corrects, deters one from base behavior.
Seeing good, he is pleasant. Seeing bad, he is unpleasant.

6.2

Do not choose vulgar companions.
Do not associate with low people.
Associate with noble companions and worthy friends.

6.3

One who drinks deeply of Dhamma
rests at ease with a clear mind.
The sage delights always in Dhamma—
the great noble Truth.

6.4

Irrigators straighten water.
Fletchers straighten arrows.
Carpenters straighten lumber.
The sage straightens himself.

6.5

Like a boulder in the wind,
the sage is not stirred by praise or blame.

6.6

Like a deep, still lake,
the sage is clear in the presence of Dhamma.

6.7

The realized man is attached to nothing.
The wise do not make small talk for enjoyment.
Sometimes visited by pleasure, sometimes visited by pain,
the sage is neither elated nor depressed.

6.8

Do not for your own or for another's sake
crave children, wealth or empire.
Do not pursue prosperity at all costs.
Be virtuous, noble, wise.

6.9

Few in this world cross to the far shore.
The multitudes scurry back and forth on the near bank.
6.10

Only those who live Dhamma cross to the far shore.
It is difficult to break free of death.
6.11

The sage turns his back on darkness and walks in light.
Moving from the familiar to no place at all,
he lives a solitude few can enjoy.
6.12

And there he finds bliss.
Free of possessions, free of desire,
free of all that clouds the mind.
6.13

One whose mind has been stilled by Awareness,
who enjoys with indifference freedom from bondage,
who is pure and radiant in this realm of dark passion—
such a one, even in mortal life,
has realized Nirvana.
6.14

7. The Realized

For one whose search has ended, who is free of sorrow,   7.1
who is free in every way, who is liberated from all bonds,
the fever of life has broken.

The Awakened One moves on and delights in no place.   7.2
Like a swan migrating from lake to lake,
he abandons every home.

One who knows the source of food has no desire to hoard it.   7.3
Realizing emptiness, he is free and unconditioned.
Like a bird in flight, his movements leave no trace.

One whose desires are extinguished   7.4
cares nothing even for food.
Realizing emptiness, he is free and unconditioned.
Like a bird in flight, his movements leave no trace.

To one who controls his senses as a charioteer   7.5
controls his horses, who is free of pride and obsessions,
even the gods pay homage.

Accepting as the ground of earth,   7.6
anchored as the gatepost of a city,
tranquil as a pond free of silt —
for such a one, wandering through birth and death is finished.

His thoughts are stilled. His words are stilled.   7.7
His work has come to an end.
He has realized perfection.

One who has realized the uncreated Void   7.8
has no need of faith and belief.
He has severed all bonds, broken all links and completely let go.
He is indeed supreme among men.

Whether village or forest, valley or mountain,   7.9
the Awakened One delights in where he is.

He delights in forests other people shun.   7.10
Free of preferences and passion, he delights in everything.

8. Thousands

Better than a thousand discourses full of meaningless words
is the single word of truth that brings peace.

8.1

Better than a thousand verses full of meaningless words
is the single line of truth that brings peace.

8.2

Though one recites a hundred scriptures
full of meaningless words,
better is the single utterance of Dhamma that brings peace.

8.3

Though a great warrior may conquer
a thousand-thousand men in battle,
greater still is he who conquers himself alone.

8.4

Better by far to conquer oneself rather than others.
One who triumphs in self-mastery,
one who reaches Self-realization,
neither gods nor the instruments of the gods—
not even Mara and Brahma together—
can vanquish the victory of such a one.

8.5

8.6

If month after month for a hundred years
one offered a thousand sacrifices,
and if for a single moment
another recognized a Self-realized man,
that single moment would be worth far more
than the sacrifices of a hundred years.

8.7

If for a hundred years one tended a ritual fire in the forest,
and if for a single moment
another honored a Self-realized man,
that single moment would be worth far more
than the rituals of a hundred years.

8.8

Whatever amount of sacrifices and offerings
one determined to gain merit might manage in an entire year,
would not be worth a fraction of a single moment's reverence
for one who embodies Truth.

8.9

In one with the capacity for reverence four qualities increase:
strength, beauty, happiness, and span of life.

8.10

Better than a hundred years lived in obedience to desire,
is one day lived in virtue and stillness.

8.11

Better than a hundred years lived clouded with ignorance,
is one day lived in clarity and insight.

8.12

Better than a hundred years lived in lethargy and sloth,
is one day lived with vitality and purpose.

8.13

Better than a hundred years lived not witnessing
the arising and passing away of Creation,
is one day lived witnessing
the arising and passing away.

8.14

Better than a hundred years lived
not knowing the deathless state,
is one day lived in deathlessness.

8.15

Better than a hundred years lived unaware of ultimate Truth,
is one day lived in Awareness.

8.16

9. Evil

Being quick to do what is right restrains the mind from evil.
Being slow to do what is right invites evil into the mind.

9.1

One who commits wrong should not repeat it again and again.
Let him not find pleasure in it.
The habit of evil accumulates suffering.

9.2

One who does what is right should repeat it over and over.
Let it be the call of his heart.
The habit of right action accumulates blessings.

9.3

One who commits wrong may enjoy good fortune
as the consequence of his evil takes shape.
But when it has ripened, suffering will befall.

9.4

One who does what is right may suffer ill fortune
as the consequence of his goodness takes form.
But when they are ready, blessings will flow.

9.5

Do not overlook small wrongdoings, thinking,
"This does not make me evil."
Every drop of falling water helps fill the jar.
Little by little, the deluded store up evil.

9.6

Do not discount small acts of goodness, thinking,
"This does not make me good."
Every drop of falling water helps fill the jar.
Little by little, the wise store up goodness.

9.7

As a merchant's caravan avoids a treacherous road,
as one who loves life avoids drinking poison,
so should you avoid the dangers of evil.

9.8

A hand without wounds can safely carry poison.
A man not open to evil cannot be harmed by evil.

9.9

Whoever wrongs an innocent one —
one who is pure and free of fault —
will have his act turn back upon him
like dust thrown into the wind.

9.10

After death, some find themselves in a mother's womb.
Those who do evil are bound to a state of suffering.
Those who do good arise to a state of heaven.
Those unstained by either realize Nirvana.

9.11

Nowhere in this world —
not in the sky, under the sea, or in a mountain cave —
can a man escape the consequences of evil action.

9.12

Nowhere in this world —
not in the sky, under the sea, or in a mountain cave —
can a man hide from death.

9.13

10. Violence

Everyone fears pain. Everyone fears death.
Knowing others to be the same as yourself,
do not kill or cause another to kill.
          10.1

Everyone fears pain. Everyone holds life dear.
Knowing others to be the same as yourself,
do not kill or cause another to kill.
          10.2

One who hurts other beings desiring happiness
will in his own search for happiness
find it neither in life nor after death.
          10.3

One who does not hurt other beings desiring happiness
will in his own search for happiness
find it both in life and after death.
          10.4

Do not speak harshly. What you say will come back to you.
Angry words are painful and invite retaliation.
          10.5

When you are still and silent as a shattered gong,
you will know Nirvana. Anger is not possible.
          10.6

As the rod of the cowherd drives cattle,
so do old age and death drive the life of beings.
          10.7

The deluded are oblivious to their evil. The ignorant,
by their actions, ignite fires that will consume them.
          10.8

He who inflicts pain on the innocent,
quickly suffers one of ten misfortunes:
          10.9
severe pain, great loss, broken bones,
grave illness, mental derangement,
          10.10
trouble with the government, cruel slander,
loss of family, destruction of possessions,
          10.11
or fire that consumes his house.
And when his body dies, he is born into hell.
          10.12

Not nakedness, not matted hair,
not fasting, not sleeping on bare ground,
not smearing the body with dust and ash,
not squatting for days on the balls of the feet—
nothing can purify the man without faith.

10.13

Yet even though one is well adorned,
if he lives in peace and with self-restraint,
if he is pure and resolute, if he harms no living thing,
then he is a brahmin, a mendicant, a monk.

10.14

In all the world is there a man of self-shame?
Who needs no reproof, as a good horse needs no whip?

10.15

Like a good horse aware of the whip,
be earnest and determined.
With faith, virtue and energy,
with meditation and insight,
with wisdom, right action and mindfulness,
leave behind this realm of sorrow.

10.16

Irrigators guide water.
Fletchers true arrows.
Carpenters shape wood.
The wise master themselves.

10.17

11. Old Age

How can you laugh and enjoy while everything burns
with suffering, impermanence, and insubstantiality?
Enshrouded in darkness, should you not seek a lamp?

11.1

Look at your beautiful body — a painted mind-puppet!
A mass of sores held up by bones.
Wretched, full of cravings, insubstantial, impermanent.

11.2

The body wears out. It is fragile, a nesting place for disease.
Soon it will putrefy and dissolve. Life ends in death.

11.3

And when the ash-grey bones of your body
lie scattered on the ground like gourds discarded in autumn,
who will then take pleasure gazing upon it?

11.4

Your body is a city of bones plastered with flesh and blood.
And in this city dwells pride, pretense,
old age, death and decay.

11.5

Even the finest royal chariots must wear out,
just as the body must decay.
But awareness of Dhamma does not perish.
Those who are Aware, instruct noble listeners.

11.6

The uninstructed man grows old like an ox.
His bulk increases but his insight does not.

11.7

For how many lives have I searched in vain
for the builder of this house?
To be born again and again is misery.

11.8

Builder of this house, you are seen!
You shall not build this house again!
The rafters are broken, the ridgepole is destroyed.
The mind is empty of illusion.
Desire is extinguished.

11.9

Those who do not seek Truth while young,
who do not gain the true treasure of life,
later ruminate with regret
like old herons on a pond with no fish.

Those who do not seek Truth while young,
who do not gain the true treasure of life,
lie like spent arrows that missed the mark,
brooding over what went wrong.

11.10

11.11

12. Self

One who holds the self dear must guard it well.
Of the three night watches, one should be spent wide awake. 12.1

Become established in virtue yourself
before preaching to others.
In this way, the sage avoids error. 12.2

Whatever you preach to others,
do accordingly yourself.
Self-mastery is not easy. 12.3

Only the self can save the self.
What other savior could there be?
When self and savior are one,
self-mastery is accomplished. 12.4

The evil you do is yours alone.
It is born of you, enacted by you.
Evil grinds the ignorant like a diamond grinds a weaker stone. 12.5

The evil you do spreads over you,
like a parasitic vine choking a tree.
The ignorant bring upon themselves
what only their worst enemies might wish for them. 12.6

Doing what is wrong and harmful to oneself comes naturally.
Doing what is right and beneficial takes effort. 12.7

The ignorant man, who clings to delusion
and mocks the teaching of Dhamma,
is destroyed by the outcome of his ignorance,
like a reed that dies when its fruit ripens. 12.8

It is you who commits evil, and you who are defiled by it.
It is you who abstains from evil and are purified.
Purity and defilement are in your hands.
No one can purify another. 12.9

Do not abandon self-purpose for the purpose of another,
no matter how great it seems.
When you perceive self-purpose,
devote yourself wholly to it.

12.10

13. The World

Do not live a base life.
Do not live a careless life.
Do not live a false life.
Do not inflate the world.

13.1

Arise! Wake up! Live the virtue of Dhamma.
One who lives Dhamma dwells in contentment,
both in this world and beyond.

13.2

Live the virtue of Dhamma. Do not fail to practice.
One who lives Dhamma dwells in contentment,
both in this world and beyond.

13.3

One who sees the world is a bubble, a mirage,
cannot be seen by the Lord of Death.

13.4

See the world as it is —
a gaudy chariot that captivates the foolish!
The wise have no interest.

13.5

Whoever overcomes delusion and becomes Aware,
illuminates the world like the moon coming free of a cloud.

13.6

Whoever overcomes ignorance and performs right action,
illuminates the world like the moon coming free of a cloud.

13.7

People are blind. Few come to see clearly.
People are like birds caught in a net.
Few escape to freedom.

13.8

Swans follow the path of the sun,
moving through space by virtue of unseen powers.
The wise drift free of the world,
no longer bound by the illusions of Mara.

13.9

Truth is the first principle. 13.10
One who speaks what he knows is not true,
giving no thought to the world beyond,
is capable of all other evil.

The ignorant are not inclined to generosity. 13.11
The selfish do not go to heaven.
The wise are fulfilled by giving and find joy in heaven.

Better than reigning supreme on earth, 13.12
better than going to heaven, better than ruling the universe,
is entering the stream of Nirvana.

14. The Awakened

14.1

The Awakened One's state cannot be overturned.
None can assail it.
Down what path can you lead one
who abides in the pathless infinite?

14.2

The Awakened One is not ensnared, entangled,
or full of cravings. He cannot be threatened or enticed.
Down what path can you lead one
who abides in the pathless infinite?

14.3

One who is awake and mindful, who abides in stillness,
who delights in the freedom of non-attachment—
even the gods envy such a one.

14.4

It is a rare event to be born human.
Mortal life is difficult.
It is a rare opportunity to hear Dhamma.
Buddhas do not often appear.

14.5

To do no evil, to perform right action, to purify the mind—
this is what the Buddhas teach.

14.6

Patience is the highest virtue.
Nirvana is the highest goal.
So say the Awakened Ones.
One who harms others has not even started.
One who inflicts injury has not begun to practice.

14.7

Speak no evil.
Do no harm.
Practice self-mastery.
Eat in moderation.
Dwell in solitude.
Abide in higher states.
This is what the Buddhas teach.

Even a shower of gold could not satisfy your cravings
and desires, could not free you from pleasure and pain.

14.8

The sage does not desire even divine pleasures.
One who delights in the absence of desire
has realized the teaching of the Buddhas.

14.9

In their fear, many flee to mountains and forests,
seeking sanctuary in groves and trees.

14.10

This is not a secure sanctuary.
This is not an adequate refuge.
It offers no release from suffering.

14.11

Whoever seeks refuge in the Buddha, the Dhamma,
and the Sangha realizes these four noble truths:

14.12

Life is suffering.
Suffering has a cause.
There is a way to end suffering.
The noble eightfold path is the way.

14.13

This is the secure refuge.
This is the ultimate sanctuary.
One who takes refuge here is released from all suffering.

14.14

The appearance of an Awakened One is rare.
One does not turn up just anywhere.
Those who live in the same place and time are fortunate.

14.15

Blessed is the Way of Buddha.
Blessed is the Truth of Dhamma.
Blessed is the Life of Sangha.
Blessed are the efforts of earnest disciples.

14.16

The fortunate virtue of one who recognizes the worthy,   14.17
whether Buddhas or wise disciples,
who recognizes those who are free of evil and delusion,
who recognizes those who are not bound by suffering —
the fortunate virtue of such a one as this   14.18
cannot be understood by saying it is this much or that much.

15. Contentment

Truly, we dwell in contentment.
Surrounded by hatred, we feel no hate.
Living among those who hate, we do not abide in hatred.

15.1

Truly, we dwell in contentment.
Surrounded by sickness, we are not sick.
Living among the sick, we are free of sickness.

15.2

Truly, we dwell in contentment.
Surrounded by restlessness, we are not restless.
Living among the restless, we abide in stillness.

15.3

Truly, we dwell in contentment. We have nothing.
We are nourished by bliss like the radiant gods.

15.4

Victory causes hatred. The defeated dream of revenge.
One who has given up victory and defeat can sleep in peace.

15.5

Nothing burns like desire.
There is no greater evil than hate.
Nothing is so painful as existing in a body.
There is no greater joy than Nirvana.

15.6

Craving is the worst disease.
Material existence is the worst suffering.
Knowing this is the way it is,
one realizes the bliss of Nirvana.

15.7

Health is the greatest attribute.
Contentment is the greatest treasure.
Trust is the greatest kinsman.
Nirvana is the highest bliss.

15.8

Having embraced solitude and stillness,
having been released from fear and delusion,
one realizes the rapture of Dhamma.

15.9

It is good to associate with the wise.   15.10
To be in their presence is always a delight.
To never suffer the presence of fools is also a delight.

One who associates with fools walks a long road of sorrow.   15.11
Being with a fool is like being with an enemy.
Being with a sage is like being with a beloved kinsman.

So if you meet someone who is aware, insightful, wise,   15.12
someone of enduring virtue, devotion, and nobility,
someone clear and real—
follow such a one as the moon follows the earth.

16. Pleasure

One who does what is wrong and fails to do what is right, 16.1
who pursues sense pleasures and ignores the path of truth,
will one day meet a man who pursues Truth
and be filled with envy.

Do not attach your thoughts 16.2
to the desirable or the undesirable.
To not have what you think is desirable causes suffering.
To have what you think is undesirable causes suffering.

Therefore, do not bind yourself to pleasure. 16.3
Separation from the desirable is experienced as pain.
One who sees nothing as desirable or undesirable
is bound to nothing.

Desire causes suffering and fear. 16.4
One who is free of desire is free of suffering.
Where is the cause of fear?

Caring causes suffering and fear. 16.5
One who is free of caring is free of suffering.
Where is the cause of fear?

Pleasure causes suffering and fear. 16.6
One who is free of pleasure is free of suffering.
Where is the cause of fear?

Passion causes suffering and fear. 16.7
One who is free of passion is free of suffering.
Where is the cause of fear?

Craving causes suffering and fear. 16.8
One who is free of craving is free of suffering.
Where is the cause of fear?

One who is established in clarity and virtue,   16.9
one who lives Dhamma and speaks the truth,
one who does what is his alone to do —
such a one is beloved in the world.

One who aspires to the Unknowable,   16.10
whose mind is clear and determined,
whose heart is not bound to sense pleasures,
is called "one who goes upstream."

When one returns home after a long journey   16.11
he is greeted with joy by relatives, friends, and well-wishers.

In the same way, when one travels from this world to the next,   16.12
he is welcomed by his good deeds,
like a loved one returning to kinsmen.

17. Anger

Give up anger. Surrender pride. Cut all ties and bindings.
Misery cannot befall one who is bereft of possessions,
who is unattached to name and form.

17.1

One who can hold back arisen anger as if controlling
a runaway chariot, I call a charioteer.
Others merely clutch the reins.

17.2

Overcome anger with no-anger.
Overcome evil with goodness.
Overcome selfishness with generosity.
Overcome falseness with truth.

17.3

Speak the truth. Refrain from anger.
Give when asked, even if you have little.
By these three traits one knows the presence
of the radiant gods.

17.4

The wise ones, who do no harm,
who restrain the body, mind and senses,
enter the immutable abode, and having entered,
grieve no more.

17.5

Those who are ever-wakeful,
who observe the Way day and night,
who are wholly intent on Nirvana,
cease to be intoxicated by illusion.

17.6

It is an old saying, Atula, nothing new:
"They criticize one who sits in silence.
They criticize one who talks too much.
They criticize one who talks in moderation."
No one in this world escapes being criticized.

17.7

There never was and never will be —
nor is there existing now —
a person wholly criticized or wholly praised.

17.8

But who dares criticize one who day after day is observed
to live impeccably, who is intelligent, wise,
and established in virtue?

17.9

He is as pure as a coin of Jambunada gold.
The wise praise him. The radiant gods praise him.
By Brahma himself he is praised.

17.10

Guard against anger in the body.
Be patient and refrain from harmful deeds.
Practice right action.

17.11

Guard against anger in speech.
Be patient and refrain from harmful words.
Practice right speaking.

17.12

Guard against anger in the mind.
Be patient and refrain from harmful thoughts.
Practice right thinking.

17.13

The wise ones,
who are self-controlled in body, speech, and mind,
are indeed masters of themselves.

17.14

18. Impurity

Your life is now a withered yellow leaf.   18.1
Mara's minions of death approach.
You stand on the brink of departure,
yet have made no preparations for the journey.

Become a lamp unto yourself.   18.2
Begin now. Work in earnest.
Become clear and aware.
Cleansed of impurities, returned to innocence,
you will enter the realm of the great.

Your life is at an end.   18.3
Death stands before you.
There is no reprieve.
Yet you have made no preparations for the journey.

Become a lamp unto yourself.   18.4
Begin now. Work in earnest.
Become clear and aware.
Cleansed of impurities, returned to innocence,
you will not suffer birth and old age again.

The wise remove their own impurities carefully,   18.5
little by little, moment by moment,
like a silversmith removing impurities from silver.

Just as rust corrodes the iron that produced it,   18.6
so do impure actions bring one to a miserable state.

Scriptures corrode when not recited.   18.7
Houses corrode when not repaired.
Sloth corrodes physical beauty.
Negligence corrodes the watchful.

Transgression corrodes a woman's femininity.
Stinginess corrodes a man's generosity.
Impure actions are corrosive,
both in this world and beyond.

18.8

The greatest of all impurities is ignorance —
the supreme impurity. Remove the impurity of ignorance
and become immaculate, you who practice Dhamma.

18.9

It is easy to live a shameless life — impudent as a crow,
agressive, arrogant, selfish, disparaging, corrupt.

18.10

It is hard to live a mindful life — sensitive to shame,
striving for purity, selfless, discerning, sincere.

18.11

Whoever in this world destroys life, tells lies,
who takes what is not given, who goes to the wife of another,
who gives himself up to intoxicants —
that man chops at the very source of himself.

18.12

18.13

Know this, my friend: Impure actions carry forward.
Do not let greed and ignorance
sentence you to long-term suffering.

18.14

People give alms according to their beliefs and pleasure.
One who becomes upset about the food and drink
he does or does not receive, will never attain stillness,
be it day or night.

18.15

But one in whom judgment and self-interest have been cut out,
destroyed at the root, will attain stillness,
be it day or night.

18.16

No fire burns like lust.
No chains imprison like hate.
No net ensnares like delusion.
No river torrents like desire.

18.17

It is easy to see the faults of others, difficult to see one's own. 18.18
You expose the faults of others as one winnowing chaff,
yet hide your own like a dishonest gambler
concealing a bad throw of the dice.

One who constantly judges the faults of others, 18.19
always taking offense, suffers an increase in his own impurities,
and grows ever farther away from the end of ignorance.

There is no path through emptiness. 18.20
There is no refuge outside Dhamma.
Ordinary men delight in complex illusions.
The Awakened are free of illusion.

There is no path through emptiness. 18.21
There is no refuge outside Dhamma.
The created world is not eternal.
The Awakened are not impatient.

19. Established in Virtue

One who forces an issue for his own benefit 19.1
is not established in virtue.
But the wise one, who considers an issue from all sides,
who guides others without force, 19.2
who follows eternal principles,
is said to be established in virtue.

A man is not wise because he talks a lot. 19.3
One who is self-secure, who is without enmity or fear,
is said to be wise.

A man is not a bearer of the teaching 19.4
because he makes learned speeches.
One who learns but little, yet realizes Dhamma
in the body of self and lives true to it,
is indeed a bearer of the teaching.

A man is not a venerable elder because his hair turns grey. 19.5
One who has ripened in years only
is said to have "grown old in vain."

One who embodies truth, virtue, 19.6
harmlessness, restraint, and self-mastery,
who is free of impurities and rich in wisdom,
is called a venerable elder.

Not by mere talk nor physical beauty can an envious, 19.7
greedy, deceitful man become a man of virtue.

One in whom these impurities are cut off, dispelled, 19.8
destroyed at the root, who is wise and free of enmity,
is called a man of virtue.

Not by merely shaving his head can a dishonest, 19.9
undisciplined man become a renunciant.
How can one full of cravings and greed be a renunciant?

But one who stills all evils in himself, coarse or subtle,   19.10
in every way can be called a renunciant.

Not merely by begging from others   19.11
does one become a simple mendicant.
Nor does one become a mendicant by living a grosser life.

But one who lives a life of virtue,   19.12
who gives no thought to good and evil,
who moves about the world with indifference,
is indeed a mendicant.

Not merely by observing silence   19.13
does a confused and ignorant man become a sage.
But the wise one who, as if holding up a set of scales,
selects what is true
and rejects what is false, is called a sage.   19.14
This is the reason he is a sage.
He knows both worlds, and so is called a sage.

One who harms living beings is not noble.   19.15
One who is harmless to living beings is called noble.

Not with rules or rituals, not with learning or higher states,   19.16
not with sleeping alone, or thinking:
"I enjoy the peace of renunciation unknown by ordinary men,"
should the seeker be content until self-will is extinguished.

20. The Way

The best way is the eightfold path.
The best sayings are the four noble truths.
The best quality is detachment.
The best being on two legs is one who sees clearly.

20.1

There is one Way, no other.
It leads to the vision of Truth.
Enter the Way.
Mara the Beguiler will lose sight of you.

20.2

The Way puts an end to suffering.
I proclaim the Way, having known myself
the extrication of the arrows.

20.3

All effort must be made by you alone.
Buddhas only point the path.
Enter the Way.
Become absorbed in Awareness.
Break free of the bonds of Mara.

20.4

"All of Creation is transient."
When one sees clearly this truth, he is done with suffering.
This is the path to pure Awareness.

20.5

"All of Creation is sorrow."
When one sees clearly this truth, he is done with suffering.
This is the path to pure Awareness.

20.6

"All of Creation is not Self."
When one sees clearly this truth, he is done with suffering.
This is the path to pure Awareness.

20.7

One who is indolent when it is time for effort—
who, though young and strong, is lazy, weak-willed,
and lacking in determination—will never find the Way.

20.8

Guard your speech.
Observe your mind.
Do no harm with your body.
Practice these three and you walk the path of the masters.

20.9

Clarity increases through spiritual practice.
Clarity weakens with lack of practice.
Knowing this two-way path of gain and loss,
walk in the direction of clarity.

20.10

Cut down the jungle of desire, not just a tree.
From the jungle of desire comes fear.
Cut down the jungle of desire, you practitioners,
and cut out the underbrush of lust. Be free of the jungle.

20.11

For if the least bit of underbrush remains
of the desire between man and woman,
you are bound to delusion like a suckling calf to its mother.

20.12

Root out your love of self
as you would pull up a faded autumn lotus.
Cherish only the path of peace that leads to Nirvana.
Be guided by One Who Is Gone.

20.13

"I will live here in monsoon season,
and there during the hot and cold months."
Lost in such thoughts, the unaware ignore what awaits.

20.14

Infatuated with children and cattle,
the unaware man is swept away by death,
as a flood carries off a sleeping village.

20.15

Children are no refuge.
Fathers and mothers and families are no refuge.
When death takes hold, kinsmen cannot protect you.

20.16

Understanding the import of this,
the wise act in accordance with virtue,
and quickly clear the way to Nirvana.

20.17

21. Miscellany

If by giving up a lesser happiness
one would enjoy a greater happiness,
the wise would surely give up the lesser and enjoy the greater.

21.1

One who seeks his own pleasure while inflicting misery
on others, is entangled in hostility and not freed from hate.

21.2

By not doing what needs to be done,
and doing what should not be done,
the proud and insolent man increases his burden of defilements.

21.3

But defilement comes to an end
for one who is mindful of the nature of the body,
who does not do what should not be done,
and who does what needs to be done.

21.4

Having slain mother, father, and two warrior kings,
having ravaged a kingdom and slain its people,
the brahmin, untouched, moves on.

21.5

Having slain mother, father, two wise kings,
and a tiger as the fifth, the brahmin, untouched, moves on.

21.6

Wide awake, the disciples of Gotama arise at every watch.
Day and night they are mindful of Buddha.

21.7

Wide awake, the disciples of Gotama arise at every watch.
Day and night they are mindful of Dhamma.

21.8

Wide awake, the disciples of Gotama arise at every watch.
Day and night they are mindful of Sangha.

21.9

Wide awake, the disciples of Gotama arise at every watch.
Day and night they are mindful of the senses.

21.10

Wide awake, the disciples of Gotama arise at every watch.
Day and night the mind delights in harmlessness.

21.11

Wide awake, the disciples of Gotama arise at every watch.   21.12
Day and night the mind delights in meditation.

It is painful to go forth into homelessness,   21.13
difficult to find joy in it.
It is painful to live in a household,
difficult to be alone among many.
The traveler of life and death is trapped in misery.
Cease traveling. Escape misery.

A man of faith, established in virtue,   21.14
who is possessed of wealth and fame —
such a man is honored wherever he goes.

Like the snow-capped Himalayas,   21.15
good people shine from afar.
Like arrows shot into the night,
the evil ones are swallowed by darkness.

Sitting alone, sleeping alone,   21.16
walking alone without tiring —
one who has tamed himself, alone,
delights in the solitude of the forest.

22. Hell

He who speaks what is not true goes to hell.
He who denies what he has done also goes to hell.
Both sin against Truth, and pass through death
into an equally woeful state.

22.1

Many even who wear the saffron robe
are evil-minded and unrestrained.
These evil ones, by their evil deeds,
pass through death into a woeful state.

22.2

Better to swallow a red-hot ball of iron
than to be an evil, undisciplined monk
feeding on the alms of the devout.

22.3

The heedless man who pursues another's wife
suffers four misfortunes: acquisition of demerit, disturbed sleep,
disgrace is the third, the fourth is birth into hell.

22.4

Acquisition of demerit and a wretched future
in exchange for the brief delight of the frightened
lying in the arms of the frightened.
The king also imposes harsh penalties.
Therefore, do not pursue the wife of another.

22.5

Just as kusa grass held wrongly can cut the hand,
so a practitioner's life lived badly can drag him into hell.

22.6

Acts done absently, practices not observed,
dubious spiritual vows — these bear little fruit.

22.7

With any undertaking, give yourself to it wholly.
The half-hearted practitioner
succeeds only in stirring up more dust.

22.8

A bad deed is best left undone. Bad deeds torment one later.
A good deed brings no regret and so should be performed.

22.9

Like a frontier town, fortified inside and out, fortify yourself. 22.10
Do not let the moment pass.
Those who let their moment pass grieve in hell.

Ashamed of what is not shameful, 22.11
unashamed of what is shameful,
those who are unaware of Truth fall into a state of misery.

Fearing what is not fearful, unafraid of what should be feared, 22.12
those who are unaware of Truth fall into a state of misery.

Finding fault with what is right, 22.13
finding no fault with what is wrong,
those who are unaware of Truth fall into a state of misery.

Seeing what is right is right, seeing what is wrong is wrong, 22.14
those aware of Truth find the fortunate state.

23. The Elephant

I endure in silence the harsh words of others
as a battle elephant endures arrows from the bow.
Many people are ill-behaved.

23.1

Only trained elephants are ridden in battle.
Only trained elephants are ridden by kings.
The best of men have trained themselves
to endure harsh words in silence.

23.2

Tamed mules are excellent. So are the thoroughbred horses
of Sindh and the tusked battle elephants.
Best of all is the self-tamed man.

23.3

For it is not by these animals
that one goes to the Place Not Gone To,
but by the self-tamed, well-trained, disciplined self.

23.4

The elephant called "Guardian of the Treasure"
is hard to control when in rut.
Tied up, the tusker won't eat a morsel,
yearning for the grove of elephants.

23.5

The sluggard who eats too much and sleeps too much,
who rolls about like an overfed hog,
is reborn again and again in ignorance.

23.6

This mind once wandered where it pleased,
as it pleased, according to whim.
Now I control its movements,
as the holder of the hooked staff controls the rutting elephant.

23.7

Delight in Awareness. Observe the mind.
Pull yourself out of misery like an elephant climbing from mud.

23.8

If one should meet a mature friend,
a fellow traveler, a wise companion,
go with that one, overcoming all obstacles, mindful and happy.

23.9

If one does not meet a mature friend,
a fellow traveler, a wise companion,
go the way alone, like a king leaving a conquered land,
like an elephant in the Matanga forest.

23.10

Better a life of solitude.
The deluded are not fit companions.
Travel the way alone, at ease, doing no harm,
like an elephant in the Matanga forest.

23.11

Having friends when you need them is a blessing.
Being content with what is, is a blessing.
A good deed as your last act is a blessing.
The surrendering of all sorrow is a blessing.

23.12

Reverence for the mother is a blessing in the world.
Reverence for the father is also a blessing.
Reverence for the practitioner is a blessing in the world.
Reverence for the brahmin is also a blessing.

23.13

Lifelong virtue is a blessing.
Faith is a blessing.
Wisdom is a blessing.
Refraining from harm is a blessing.

23.14

24. Craving

The cravings of the careless man grow like a clinging vine. 24.1
He jumps from experience to experience
like a monkey seeking fruit in the forest.

When a man is overcome by miserable, clinging cravings, 24.2
his sorrows grow like rain-soaked grass.

When a man overcomes his miserable, clinging cravings, 24.3
sorrows fall away like raindrops from a lotus.

I tell you this—and you who are gathered 24.4
have the good fortune to hear it:
Dig up desire by the root, as you would birana grass.
Do not let Mara break you again and again,
as a river breaks reeds in a flood.

Cut down a tree and it will grow back if the root 24.5
is undamaged and strong. So too will suffering
arise again and again if the root of craving is not destroyed.

One in whom the thirty-six streams of experience 24.6
flow mightily towards pleasure cannot see rightly,
and is swept away by currents of lustful intent.

The streams flow everywhere. 24.7
Clinging vines sprout everywhere.
Seeing the vine sprout up,
sever its root with the blade of insight.

Beings experience pleasing sensations. 24.8
Craving pleasure, one is bound to pleasure.
Being bound to pleasure, one is bound to birth and death.

Driven by desire, the mass of men 24.9
scurry about like a hunted hare.
Bound by their clingings and attachments,
they suffer and suffer for a very long time.

Driven by desire, the mass of men
scurry about like a hunted hare.
Therefore, let the practitioner drive out desire
and seek the freedom of dispassion.

One who is free of the jungle of desire
yet still attached to desire, will, though free,
return to the jungle and re-enter bondage.

Bindings of iron, wood or rope
are not called strong by the wise.
Attraction to jewels and finery, affection for wives and children,
these are strong bindings, say the wise.
Though supple, they drag one down and are hard to loosen.
Some men simply cut them,
renounce the world of sensory delights,
and follow the Way without a backward glance.

Those who are attached to desire return to the stream
of experience, as a spider returns to the center of its web.
The wise sever all attachments,
and free from craving, leave suffering behind.

Hold no thought of future.
Hold no thought of past.
Hold no thought of a moment between.
Transcend experience and cross over.
You are finished with birth and death.

For one gripped by restless thoughts,
whose cravings are acute, who seeks only pleasure,
desire grows all the more as he draws his fetters tighter.

But one who delights in stilling thought, who is ever mindful,
who meditates on the sorrows of experience —
that one will surely break the bonds of Mara.

24.10

24.11

24.12

24.13

24.14

24.15

24.16

24.17

For one who has reached the goal,
who is fearless, desireless, unclouded,
who has plucked out the arrows of experience,
this is the final body.

24.18

Free of desire and attachment,
well-versed in language and expression,
skilled in the teaching of meaning within meaning,
one is called "wise" and "great" and "bearer of the final body."

24.19

All-conquering, all-knowing, I Am.
Touched by nothing, released of everything,
absent of desire, I am free.
Having realized I alone Am,
to whom should I attribute this?

24.20

The gift of Dhamma surpasses all gifts.
The taste of Dhamma surpasses all flavors.
The joy of Dhamma surpasses all joys.
The dissolution of desire removes all sorrows.

24.21

Wealth destroys the ignorant, but not those seeking beyond.
Craving wealth, the ignorant man
destroys himself and those around him.

24.22

Weeds make fields unsuitable for seeding.
Greed makes people unsuitable to receive.
Hence, what is given to those free of greed
bears the most abundant fruit.

24.23

Weeds make fields unsuitable for seeding.
Hatred makes people unsuitable to receive.
Hence, what is given to those free of hate
bears the most abundant fruit.

24.24

Weeds make fields unsuitable for seeding.
Delusion makes people unsuitable to receive.
Hence, what is given to those free of delusion
bears the most abundant fruit.

24.25

Weeds make fields unsuitable for seeding.
Desire makes people unsuitable to receive.
Hence, what is given to those free of desire
bears the most abundant fruit.

24.26

25. The Practitioner

25.1

Restraining the eye is good. It is good to restrain the ear.
Restraining the nose is good. It is good to restrain the tongue.

25.2

Restraint of the body is good.
It is good to restrain one's speech.
Restraint of the mind is good.
It is good to be restrained in all things.
Being restrained in all things,
the practitioner is released from suffering.

25.3

One with hands restrained,
feet restrained, speech restrained,
one who exercises the utmost restraint,
one who delights in introspection,
who is composed, solitary and content—
such a one is known as a practitioner.

25.4

The practitioner who controls his speech,
who talks in moderation without arrogance or conceit,
who illuminates the goal and spirit of Dhamma—
sweet indeed are his words.

25.5

Abiding in Dhamma, delighting in Dhamma,
reflecting on Dhamma, remembering Dhamma,
the practitioner will not fall away from Dhamma.

25.6

Do not be discontent with what you are given,
nor envy the lot of others.
The practitioner who harbors envy
will never come to Awareness.

25.7

The practitioner who is given little yet is content,
who lives a pure and vigorous life,
is praised even by the gods.

One who observes mind and form with no sense of "mine,"
and who does not yearn for what is not,
is a true practitioner.

25.8

The practitioner who lives in love and kindness,
who walks the Way of Buddha, will find stillness,
subdue the phantoms of Creation, and attain bliss.

25.9

Practitioner, empty your boat!
Lightened, it will sail more quickly.
Cast off hatred and desire, and you will realize Nirvana.

25.10

Cut the five bindings.
Release the five attachments.
Cultivate the five qualities.
Transcend the five evils.
You will be called "one who has crossed the torrent."

25.11

Become absorbed in meditation, practitioner!
Do not be negligent!
Do not surrender your mind to the swirl of sense pleasures.
Do not carelessly swallow a molten ball of iron,
then cry out in torment when it burns.

25.12

One cannot become absorbed in meditation without clarity.
One cannot realize clarity without meditation.
One who meditates in clarity realizes Nirvana.

25.13

When in stillness the practitioner discovers his house is empty,
the Truth of Dhamma is clear. The joy of this is indescribable.

25.14

Witnessing the arising and passing of the manifest world,
one delights in the joy of Awareness and realizes the deathless.

25.15

The wise practitioner in this world begins by
guarding the senses, learning contentment,
practicing spiritual disciplines, and associating with
worthy friends who live pure and vigorous lives.

25.16

Form the habit of friendship.
Conduct yourself with skill.
In fulfillment find the joy without sorrow.

25.17

As the jasmine sheds withered flowers,
so should the practitioner shed desire and aversion.

25.18

The practitioner whose body is tranquil, whose speech is calm,
whose mind is stilled, who refuses the bait of worldliness,
is said to be "at peace."

25.19

You alone can motivate yourself.
You alone can examine yourself.
The practitioner who is self-observed and aware,
abides in contentment.

25.20

You are your own master.
You are your own refuge.
Train yourself as a horseman trains a fine horse.

25.21

The practitioner who is filled with delight as he walks
the Way of Buddha, will find stillness,
subdue the phantoms of Creation, and attain bliss.

25.22

Truly, even a novice practitioner who walks
the Way of Buddha, lights up the world
like the moon coming free of a cloud.

25.23

26. The Brahmin

Exert strong effort, brahmin.   26.1
Cut entirely the stream. Abandon all sense desires.
Witnessing the dissolution of Creation, perceive the uncreated.

When the brahmin has crossed over with both tranquility   26.2
and insight, then, for that one, all bonds are broken.

One for whom there is neither here nor beyond nor both,   26.3
who is free of distress, untethered, I call a "brahmin."

One who is aware, mindful, untouched by desire,   26.4
one whose work is ended, who is free of impurities,
who has realized the supreme state—such a one is a brahmin.

The sun shines by day.   26.5
The moon lights the night.
The warrior is bright in armor.
The brahmin glows in meditation.
Day and night, the Awakened One is ablaze in splendor.

One in whom ignorance has been dispelled is a brahmin.   26.6
One who lives in simple peace is an ascetic.
One who has left behind impure habits
is said to have "gone forth."

One should never strike a brahmin,   26.7
nor should a brahmin, if struck, return anger.
Shame on one who strikes a brahmin.
Greater shame on one who returns anger.

The brahmin likes nothing better   26.8
than restraining the mind from the pleasant.
When harmful thoughts are abandoned, suffering ends.

One who does no harm with body, speech, or mind,   26.9
and who in all three areas is restrained, I call a brahmin.

As the brahmin pays homage to the sacred fire,
so should homage be paid to one who teaches
the Dhamma of the Awakened One.

26.10

Not by matted hair, or ancestry, or fortunate birth
does one come to be a brahmin.
One who realizes the Truth of Dhamma is the pure one.
He is a brahmin.

26.11

You fool! What does it matter if your hair is matted?
What does it matter if you wear antelope robes?
The jungle of defilements is within you,
yet you tend the outside!

26.12

I call him brahmin who, clothed in rags, lean in body,
sits alone in the forest, absorbed in Awareness, veins showing.

26.13

I do not call one a brahmin because he was born
to a brahmin family, sprung from a brahmin womb.
He may be just a proud fool with possessions.
I call him a Brahmin who is bereft of possessions
and attached to nothing.

26.14

I call him a brahmin who has cut himself free from bondage
and does not tremble,
who has unburdened himself of attachments.

26.15

I call him a brahmin who has cut the strap of hate
and thong of greed, who has severed the cord of delusion
and bridle of bias, who has lifted the bar of ignorance
and realized Truth.

26.16

I call him a brahmin who endures without anger,
abuse, torture, imprisonment,
whose forbearance is as strong as an army.

26.17

I call him a brahmin who is without anger and devoted
to practice, who is virtuous, restrained, free of craving,
who is a bearer of the final body.

26.18

I call him a brahmin who, like a raindrop on a lotus leaf,
like a mustard seed on the point of an awl,
does not cling to sensual pleasure.

26.19

I call him a brahmin who even in this life has ceased to suffer,
who has laid down the burden, who is freed from bondage.

26.20

I call him a brahmin who is possessed of wisdom and clarity,
who sees the Way and the not-Way,
who has realized the supreme state.

26.21

I call him a brahmin who associates with neither
householders nor renunciants, who lives without shelter,
indifferent, desiring nothing.

26.22

I call him a brahmin who has laid down his rod
and renounced violence,
who is harmless to beings, both animal and rooted,
who neither kills nor causes others to kill.

26.23

I call him a brahmin who is harmonious among the hostile,
serene among the violent, detached among the clinging.

26.24

I call him a brahmin from whom desire, hatred,
pride and hypocrisy have fallen away,
like a mustard seed from the point of an awl.

26.25

I call him a brahmin who speaks only what is instructive,
useful and true, who offers offense to no one.

26.26

I call him a brahmin who in this world takes nothing
that is not given, whether long or short, small or great,
pleasant or unpleasant.

26.27

I call him a brahmin who has no yearnings for this world
or another, who is untethered, aloof, indifferent.

26.28

I call him a brahmin who is attached to nothing,
whose clarity has dispelled all doubt,
who has realized deathlessness. 26.29

I call him a brahmin who is beyond good and evil,
who is free of sorrow, immaculate, pure. 26.30

I call him a brahmin who is clear and pure as the moon,
serene, tranquil, who is no longer delighted by existence. 26.31

I call him a brahmin who has passed through this quagmire
of existence and gone beyond the swirl of illusion,
who abides in Awareness, free of craving and doubt,
who has crossed the torrential river and rests on the far shore. 26.32

I call him a brahmin who wanders homeless,
sense desires extinguished,
whose desire for sensory existence is exhausted. 26.33

I call him a brahmin who wanders homeless,
feverish cravings extinguished,
whose craving for conditioned existence is extinct. 26.34

I call him a brahmin who is free of all bondage,
who has abandoned the bondage of birth
and transcended the bondage of heaven. 26.35

I call him a brahmin who is free of preferences and aversions,
who is cool and indifferent to Creation —
a hero who conquers every world. 26.36

I call him a brahmin who sees clearly the arising
and passing away, who is unattached, well-gone, Awakened. 26.37

I call him a brahmin whose destiny is unknown to mortals,
guardians, or gods, who is pure and immaculate — an *arahant*. 26.38

I call him a brahmin for whom there is no future, no past,
no moment in between, who has nothing, wants nothing. 26.39

I call him a brahmin who is a powerful bull—
splendid, heroic—who is a great sage,
a victorious conqueror,
who is desireless, washed clean, Awake.

26.40

I call him a brahmin who knows other lives,
who knows heaven and the realms of woe,
who has reached the end of birth and death,
who has realized the supreme state,
who is in all ways, perfect.

26.41

Book of Yeshua
Sayings of Jesus Christ

The story of the life and death of Jesus of Nazareth is one of the most familiar in history, and his sayings have formed the basis for one of the world's great religions. It is said that Jesus' ministry began when he was thirty and lasted one to three years, during which time he traveled from place to place, teaching wherever people would listen, healing whenever they asked. It ended with his death upon a wooden cross.

The inner teachings of Jesus share a deep similarity with the enlightenment teachings of Buddha and other eastern sages. To account for this, some scholars speculate that Jesus spent his twenties in India. Perhaps. But regardless, the more fundamental reason these teachings sound similar is because they arise from, and point to, the same Truth.

Christian mystics like Saint John of the Cross and Meister Eckhart experienced firsthand the truth of this teaching, and wrote about the wonder of discovering that, as Eckhart puts it, "The eye with which I see God is the same eye with which God sees me." Or as Jesus says, "He who knows himself, at the same time knows the Totality of the All."

Yeshua is Jesus' name in his native Aramaic. *Book of Yeshua* is one of the forty-two sermons found in my book *Christ Sutras: The Complete Sayings of Jesus from All Sources Arranged as Sermons*, which contains all the sayings of Jesus from the New Testament, Gnostic Gospels, and all other early Christian writings. It is a sermon that conveys the highest teachings of Jesus in his own words, teachings that point directly to the realization of Truth. The verses used in *Book of Yeshua* are duplicated from other *Christ Sutras* sermons. The *Christ Sutras* verse numbers have been retained here to avoid confusion.

Peace to you. My peace I give to you.   42.1

It is necessary I speak to you of certain things,   42.2
because this is the teaching for the perfect.
If you desire to become perfect, you must observe these things.
If not, you shall remain ignorant.

It is impossible for a wise man to dwell with a fool.   42.3
For the wise man is perfect in all wisdom,
while the fool cannot even discern between good and bad.
The wise man is nourished by Truth,
like a tree growing by a meandering stream.

The ignorant, although they have wings, are attracted   42.4
to the visible forms, things that are far from Truth.
For that which drives them, the fire,
gives them an illusion of truth.

It shines on them with perishable beauty,   42.5
imprisons them in dark sweetness,
and captivates them with fragrant pleasure.

It blinds them with insatiable lust and burns their souls.   42.6
It becomes for them a stake in the heart
they can never dislodge. And like a bit in the mouth,
it leads them according to its own desire.

It fetters them with its chains and binds all their limbs   42.7
with the bitter bond of lust for visible things,
things that decay, and change, and swerve by impulse.

They rejoice over the concern for this life with madness   42.8
and derangement. Some pursue this derangement
without realizing their madness, thinking they are wise.

They are beguiled by the beauty of their body,   42.9
as if it would not perish, and they are frenetic.
Their thought is occupied with their deeds,
and thought is the fire that burns them.

The ignorant are always attracted downwards.   42.10
And as they are killed they are assimilated
into the substance of all beasts,
the substance of the perishable realm.

A great difference exists between the imperishable   42.11
and those who will perish.
Everything that comes from the perishable will perish,
for it comes from the perishable.
But whatever comes from the imperishable does not perish,
but itself becomes imperishable.

That flesh comes into being because of spirit is a wonder.   42.12
But if spirit came into being because of the flesh,
it would be a wonder of wonders.
Indeed, I am amazed at how the great wealth of spirit
has made its home in the great poverty of flesh.

Which falls away, flesh or spirit?   42.13
Flesh falls away.

That which you have within you will save you   42.14
if you bring it forth from yourself.
That which you do not have within you will kill you
if you do not have it within you.

All natures, all forms, all creatures exist in and with one   42.15
another, and they are resolved again into their own roots.
For the nature of matter is resolved into
the roots of its nature alone.

He who is from Truth does not die.   42.16
He who is from the womb of woman, dies.
The multitude of men go astray
because they do not know this difference. And they die.

Whoever has ears to hear about infinities, let him hear!   42.17
It is those who are awake that I address.
I come from the One that I might tell you all things.

It is to those who are worthy of my mysteries   42.18
that I tell my mysteries. Whoever finds the truth
of my words will not experience death.

My teaching is not mine, but of the One who sends me.   42.19
He who sees me, sees the One who sends me.
He who receives me, receives the One who sends me.
I come as Light into the world,
that whoever receives me may not remain in darkness.

There is light within a man of Light,   42.20
and he lights up the whole world.
If he does not shine, he is in darkness.
It is in Light that light exists.

I am Alpha and Omega, the beginning and the end.   42.21
Fear not. I am the first and the last, the Living One.
I am he who was dead, and behold, I am alive forevermore.

Before Abraham was, I am.   42.22
All authority is given me, on earth and in Heaven.
I and the Father are One.

I came to make the things below like the things above,   42.23
and the things outside like those inside.
I came to unite them in that Place.

I am the Way, the Truth, and the Life.   42.24
All who come to the Father, come through me.
If you know me, you know the Father.
Henceforth you know him, and have seen him.

It is I who am the Light above the All.   42.25
It is I who am the All.
From me does the All come forth.
Into me does the All extend.

Split a piece of wood and I am there.   42.26
Lift up a stone and you will find me.

He who will drink from my mouth will become like me,
and I myself shall become he,
and the things that are hidden shall be revealed to him.

42.27

I shall give you what no eye has seen,
and what no ear has heard, and what no hand has touched,
and what has never occurred to the human mind.

42.28

I am the Light of the world.
He who becomes as me will not walk in darkness,
but will be the Light of Life.

42.29

He who becomes as me will also do the works that I do,
and greater works than these will he do.

42.30

While you yet have time in the world,
listen to me, and I will reveal to you
the things you have pondered in your mind.

42.31

You have received mercy.
Do you not, then, desire to be filled?
Your heart is drunken.
Do you not, then, desire to be sober?

42.32

If you consider how long the world existed before you,
and how long it will exist after you,
you will find that your life is but one single day,
and your sufferings one single hour.

42.33

If you knew — you, now in this your day —
the things that make for your peace!
But they are hidden from your eyes.

42.34

While you have the Light, receive the Light,
that you may become sons of Light.

42.35

Take heed of the Living One while you are alive,
lest you die and seek to know him but be unable to do so.
He who lives from the Living One will not see death.

42.36

I know that in faith and with your whole heart   42.37
you question me. Therefore I am glad because of you.
I am truly pleased, and my Father in me rejoices
that you thus inquire and ask. Your boldness makes me
rejoice, and it affords you Life.

Inquire then, and I will tell you all you wish to know,   42.38
and I myself will make known to you what you do not ask.

II.
You ask how your end will be?   42.39
Have you discovered, then, the beginning,
that you look for the end?
Where the beginning is, there also is the end.

Blessed is he who abides in the ever-beginning.   42.40
He will know the end and will not experience death.

Blessed is He Who Is—before everything comes into being.   42.41
For He Who Is, ever has been, and ever shall be.

He Who Is, is ineffable.   42.42
No principle knows him, no authority, no subjection,
nor any creature from the foundation of the world until now,
except he alone, and anyone to whom he wills to reveal
himself through him who is from Infinite Light.
Forevermore, I offer this great Salvation.

He Who Is, is immortal and eternal, having never been born. 42.43
Everything that is born will perish.
He is unbegotten, having no beginning.
Everything that has a beginning has an end.

Because no one rules over him, he has no name.   42.44
Whatever has a name is the creation of another.
He is unperceivable. He has no form.
Whatever has form is the creation of another.

He has a semblance of his own—
not like any you have perceived or thought—
but a strange semblance that surpasses all things
and is greater than the universe.
It looks to every side and sees itself from itself.

He is infinite and ever incomprehensible.
He is unchanging good.
He is faultless. He is timeless.
He is imperishable and has no likeness to anything.
He is eternally blessed.

He is not knowable, yet he ever knows himself.
He is immeasurable. He is untraceable.
He is perfect, having no defect.
He is called, "Father of the Universe."

Before anything that now appears becomes visible,
the majesty and the authority are in the Father.
He encompasses the whole of Totality.
Nothing encompasses him.

He is all mind, and all thought, and all reflecting,
and all authority, and all will. These are equal powers.
They are the sources of Totality.

And the whole of Creation, from first to last,
is in his foreknowledge, that of the infinite, Unbegotten Father.

There comes a time and an hour when what comes next
is to go to the Father.

What must you do to be doing the work of God, the Father?
The work of God is to become as him he sends to you.

Take my yoke upon you and learn from me.
I am gentle and humble in heart,
and you will find rest for your souls.
My yoke is easy and my burden is light.

Come, follow me. I will make you fishers of men.
Come, follow me. Let the dead bury their dead.

42.54

Keep my commandments and follow my Way,
without reserve, without delay,
without respect of persons.
Walk the straight, direct, and narrow path,
and in every respect the Father will rejoice concerning you.

42.55

He who knows and keeps my commandments loves me.
He who loves me will be loved by my Father,
and I will love him and manifest myself to him.

42.56

And if you ask anything in my name, I will do it.
If you love me, therefore, keep my commandments.

42.57

The Lord our God is One.
You shall love the Lord our God with all your heart,
and with all your soul, and with all your mind,
and with all your strength.
This is the first and greatest commandment.

42.58

The second commandment is like it:
Love your neighbor as yourself.
There are no other commandments greater than these.

42.59

As I love you, therefore, love one another.
By this all men will know you are my disciples,
that you love one another.
Love your brother like your soul.
Guard him like the pupil of your eye.

42.60

Do not tell lies. Do not do what you hate.
For all things are plain in the sight of Heaven.
Nothing hidden will remain unmanifest.
Nothing covered will not be uncovered.

42.61

Do not worry about your life, about what you will eat
or what you will drink, nor about your body,
about what clothing you will put on.
Do not be concerned from morning until evening,
and from evening until morning about what you will wear.

42.62

Is not life more than food and the body more than clothing?
Look at the birds of the air. They neither sow nor reap
nor gather into barns, yet your Father in Heaven feeds them.
Are you not of more value than they?

42.63

Therefore, give no thought for tomorrow.
Let tomorrow come with tomorrow's things.
Sufficient for the day is its own arising.

42.64

Love one another and honor each other,
that continual peace may reign among you.
What you do not want done to you, that do to no one else.

42.65

Love your enemies. Do good to those who hate you.
Bless those who curse you.
Pray for those who spitefully use you.

42.66

To him who strikes you on one cheek, turn the other.
To him who takes your cloak, offer your tunic.
Give to everyone who asks, and from him who borrows
your goods, do not ask for them back.
As you want men to do to you, do to them likewise.

42.67

Be merciful, just as your Father is merciful.
Judge not, that you not be judged.
Condemn not, that you not be condemned.
Let he who is without sin cast the first stone.
Love your enemies.

42.68

For with what judgment you judge, you shall be judged,
and the measure you give will be the measure you get,
and still more will be given you.

42.69

Forgive, and you will be forgiven.
Give, and it will be given to you.
Good measure, pressed down, shaken together
and running over will be put into your bosom.

42.70

It is to the good, guileless, sincere ones
that the mystery of death is revealed.
They shall know the Kingdom of those reborn in Christ.

42.71

You must become perfect,
just as your Father in Heaven is perfect.

42.72

III.
Enter by the narrow gate.
For wide is the gate and broad is the way
that leads to destruction. And there are many who go in by it.

42.73

But strait is the gate and narrow is the way
that leads to Life. And there are few who find it.

42.74

Recognize what is in your sight,
and that which is hidden will become plain to you.
For there is nothing hidden that will not become manifest.

42.75

Come to hate falsehood and the evil of thought.
For it is thought that gives birth to falsehood,
and falsehood is far from Truth.

42.76

Ask and it shall be given you.
Seek and you shall find.
Knock and it shall be opened to you.

42.77

For everyone who asks receives, and he who seeks finds,
and to him who knocks, it will be opened.

42.78

For the one who speaks is also the one who hears,
and the one who sees is also the one who manifests,
and the one who seeks is also the one who reveals.

42.79

Let him who seeks continue seeking until he finds.
When he finds, he will become troubled,
and when he becomes troubled he will be astonished,
and he will rule over the All.

42.80

Whoever keeps my Word and follows my Way
will be a son of the Light, a son of God the Father.
It is for the sake of those who keep and do my Word
that I have come from Heaven.

42.81

Become earnest about the Word!
For as to the Word, the first part is Faith,
the second is Love, the third is Works.
From these come Life.

42.82

Whoever would become as me, let him deny himself.
Let him take up his cross and follow me.
For whoever would save his life will lose it,
but whoever loses his life for righteousness sake, will save it.
What shall it profit a man if he gain the whole world,
yet lose his own soul?

42.83

Whoever does not forsake all that he has,
is not a disciple of my Way.
Truly, he who loves his life shall lose it.
But he who renounces his life in this world
shall know eternal Life.

42.84

When you leave behind the things that cannot follow you,
then you will know peace. He who truly wants to enter
the kingdom of Heaven will enter it.

42.85

There is no one who has left house or brother or sister
or mother or father or children or land for my sake
and for the sake of Truth,
who will not receive a hundredfold, now in this time,
houses and brothers and sisters and mothers and fathers
and children and lands, and in the age to come, eternal Life.
For many who are last will be first, and the first last.

42.86

Seek ye first the kingdom of God and his righteousness,
and all these things shall be added unto you.
42.87

The kingdom of God is not found by looking out.
No one can tell you, "Look here," or "Look there."
The kingdom of God is within you.
42.88

The Kingdom will not come by waiting for it. It will not be
a matter of saying, "I found it," or "There it is."
The kingdom of God is everywhere but you do not see it!
42.89

If those who lead you say, "The kingdom of God is in the sky,"
then the birds of the sky will precede you. If they say to you,
"It is in the sea," then the fish will precede you.
Rather, the kingdom of God is inside you, and before you.
42.90

The kingdom of God is with men.
He dwells with them and they are his people.
Truly, the home of God is within you, for he is your God,
and he himself shall wipe every tear from your eyes.
42.91

Death shall be no more. Neither shall there be sorrow,
nor crying, nor suffering, nor pain,
for the former things shall all pass away.
42.92

Have faith and be of good courage.
Truly I say to you, such a rest will be yours,
where there is no eating, nor drinking, nor mourning,
nor singing, nor care, nor earthly garment, nor death.
42.93

You will no longer have your part in the lesser creation,
but will belong to the incorruptibility of the Father,
and you will not perish.
42.94

For you are in Christ always,
and Christ is always in the Father.
42.95

Until now, you have asked nothing in the name of Christ.   42.96
Ask and you will receive, that your joy may be full.
Whatever you ask in prayer, believing, you will receive.

If you can, believe! Do not fear, only believe.   42.97
All things are possible for him who believes.

Truly, if you have but faith the size of a mustard seed,   42.98
you can say to this mulberry tree, "Be pulled up by the roots
and be planted in the sea," and it would obey you.

If you have but faith as a mustard seed,   42.99
you can say to this mountain, "Move from here to there,"
and it will move. Nothing will be impossible for you.

Believe me, whoever says to this mountain, "Be taken up and   42.100
cast into the sea," and does not doubt in his heart, but believes
that what he says will come to pass, it will be done for him.

I tell you, whatever you ask in prayer,   42.101
believe that you have received it, and it will be yours.

The things that are impossible with men   42.102
are possible with God. Have faith in God.

The kingdom of God is when the two become one,   42.103
when that which is without is as that which is within,
when the male and the female are neither male nor female.

For when you make the two, one, you become a son of God.   42.104
And when you say, "Mountain, move away,"
it will move away.

To enter the Kingdom, become like an infant.   42.105
For when you make the two, one,
and make the inside like the outside,
and make the outside like the inside,
and make the above like the below,
and when you make the male and the female

one and the same, so that the male not be male,
nor the female be female,
and when you fashion an eye in place of an eye,
and a hand in place of a hand, and a foot in place of a foot,
and a likeness in place of a likeness,
then will you enter the kingdom of God.

Truly, whoever does not receive the kingdom of God   42.106
as an infant child, shall not enter it.

For the light of the body is the eye.   42.107
If, therefore, your eye is single, your whole body is light.

But if your eye is divided, being part darkness,   42.108
your whole body is darkness.
Take heed, therefore, that the light within you is not darkness.
For if the light that you are is darkness,
how great is that darkness!

He who is undivided is filled with light.   42.109
He who is divided is filled with darkness.

When you come to know yourself,   42.110
you will become what is known, and you will realize
that you are the son of the living Father.

But if you do not know yourself, you dwell in poverty,   42.111
and it is you who are that poverty.
For whoever believes he is less than the All,
is completely ignorant.

He who does not know himself knows nothing.   42.112
But he who knows himself,
at the same time knows the Totality of the All.

Heaven and earth will roll up in your presence.   42.113
For whoever finds himself, contains the world.

It is in this way that you enter the kingdom of Heaven.   42.114
But unless you receive it yourself, through direct knowing,
you will not be able to find it.

Blessed are your eyes, for they see, and your ears,   42.115
for they hear. Truly I say to you, many prophets and righteous
men have desired to see what you see, yet did not see it,
to hear what you hear, yet did not hear it.

No one will ever enter the kingdom of Heaven at my bidding,   42.116
but only because you yourself are whole.
Hearken to the Word, understand Knowledge, love Life.
No one persecutes or oppresses you other than you yourself!

Hasten to be saved without being urged!   42.117
Be eager of your own accord and, if possible,
arrive even before me. Our Father will love you.

Truly, he who receives Life and enters the Kingdom   42.118
will never leave it. Not even the Father can banish him.

Everything I have said to you,   42.119
you have heard and received in faith.
If you know these things for yourself, they are yours.
If you do not know them for yourself, they are not yours.

Be courageous and do not fear at all.   42.120
I am with you, and no enemy shall ever prevail over you.
Peace be with you. Be strong.

See rightly! The kingdom of Heaven is within you!   42.121

Heart Sutra
On Realizing Truth Beyond Wisdom

Heart of the Prajna-Paramita Sutra is the shortest and most popular sutra in Buddhism. It is said that the six hundred volumes of the *Maha Projna Sutra* are summarized by the *Diamond Sutra* in 5,000 words, and that the *Diamond Sutra* is summarized by the *Heart Sutra* in 250 words. It is considered the essence of the wisdom of Buddha, explaining perfectly the practice of non-attachment and the doctrine of emptiness. In most Buddhist monasteries and many Buddhist households, the *Heart Sutra* is recited daily.

The earliest Buddhist writings are in the Pali language, and tend to be relatively literal and logical. Later developments of Buddhism, referred to as Mahayana, were written in Sanskrit. *Heart Sutra* falls into this category.

Mahayana writings emphasize the doctrine of *sunyata* — emptiness, no-self — and use paradoxical, contradictory language designed to break down habitual beliefs and preconceptions about the nature of the world. This approach was later systemized and taken further by the Chinese Ch'an and Japanese Zen traditions, and today, the *Heart Sutra* is often chanted by Zen groups in its Japanese form *Hannya Shingyo*, both before and after a meditation sitting.

The Bodhisattva of Compassion,
having gone beyond wisdom to Truth,
saw with perfect clarity
that the five components of worldly experience —
form, sensation, perception, volition, and consciousness —
do not exist. Thus he was freed from anguish and suffering.

He said: O Seeker, form does not differ from emptiness.
Emptiness does not differ from form.
Form is emptiness. Emptiness is form.
It is the same with sensation, perception, volition, and consciousness.

All appearances are emptiness —
neither born nor unborn, neither pure nor impure,
neither arising nor passing away.

There is only emptiness.

No form, sensation, perception, volition, or consciousness.
No eyes, ears, nose, or tongue.
No body. No mind.
No sights, sounds, smells, or tastes.
No feelings. No thoughts.
No realm of the inner eye.
No realm of pure consciousness.

There is neither ignorance nor the absence of ignorance.
There is neither old age and death,
nor the absence of old age and death.
There is no suffering, no beginning, no middle, no end.
There is no path, no knowledge, no attainment.

There is nothing to attain.

The Bodhisattva abides in the Absolute, unfettered by mind.
No mind, no fear.
The imagined world is seen through. Nirvana.

All Buddhas, past, present, and future, teach one Way.
Prajna Paramita is the mantra of the Way —
the great transcendent mantra,
the brilliant, supreme, unequalled mantra
that breaks the bonds of suffering.

The mantra of Truth, not illusion.

Therefore, live this great mantra:
Gate gate paragate parasamgate bodhi svaha!

[Gone, gone, gone beyond, gone beyond beyond
to Awakening — such grace!]

Oxherding Picture Seven: The Bull Transcended

Astride the bull, I reach home.
I am serene. The bull too can rest.
The dawn has come. In blissful repose,
within my thatched dwelling,
I have abandoned the whip and rope.

All is one law, not two.
We only make the bull a temporary subject.
It is as the relation of rabbit and trap, of fish and net.
It is as gold and dross, or the moon emerging from a cloud.
One path of clear light travels on throughout endless time.

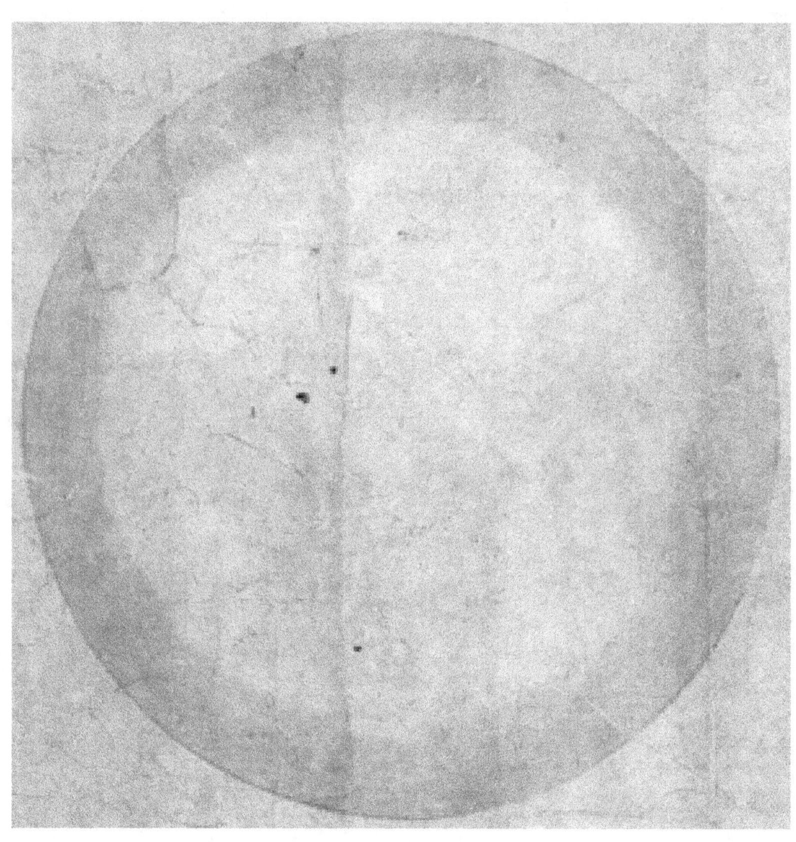

Oxherding Picture Eight: Both Bull and Self Transcended

Whip, rope, person, and bull -- all merge in No-thing.
This heaven is so vast no message can stain it.
How can a snowflake exist in raging fire?
Here are the footprints of the patriarchs.

Mediocrity is gone. Mind is clear of limitation.
I seek no state of enlightenment.
Neither do I remain where no enlightenment exists.
Since I linger in neither condition, eyes cannot see me.
If hundreds of birds strew my path with flowers,
such praise would be meaningless.

Three Books of the Absolute

Richard Rose

Richard Rose (1917–2005) was an American spiritual teacher, philosopher and poet who published several books and spoke in universities and other venues around the country during the 70's and 80's. As students began to gather around him, he turned his family farm in West Virginia into an ashram for seekers and dedicated his life to them. His teachings emphasize self-inquiry, intuition, and a deep commitment to Self-Realization.

Rose was a committed seeker himself until at the age of thirty, when, while working as a waiter in Seattle, Truth made itself known in a dramatic experience. Back on his farm a year later, he wrote a description of that occurance in a long poem, *The Three Books of the Absolute*. Though written centuries after the other texts in *The Perennial Way*, it seems to comfortably belong in their company. Mister Rose, as his students called him, was very much an "old master."

I had the privilege to call Mister Rose my teacher and friend. I was twenty years into a spiritual search and running out of hope when providence led me to him. He redefined the spiritual path for me and made "success" seem possible, even inevitable. He did that for a lot of people.

Book I

Out of the valley of the river came a wanderer.
Peace was in his eye and his soul was wrapped in Nirvana.
Peace to the wanderer.

O Eternal Essence, I was that Wanderer.
I it was who left the gardens of tranquility
that I might labor for Truth.

I sought Thee, O Eternal Essence, in grottoes and tabernacles.
I called out thy name to the stone ears of statues.
And thou answered not.

I sought Thee in the voice of nature.
I looked for Thee in the footprints of animals, in the habits of birds.
I listened for a revelation in the murmuring of waters
and the soft moaning of forests.
I laid my ear against the roaring cataracts
and bared my head to tempests.
But Thou answered not.

I have sought Thee, O Eternal Essence, within my self.
I have sought Thee in my mind until I was cursed with confusion.
And I saw Thee not.

Then, O Eternal Essence, I sought Thee whence I came.
I sought Thee in my womb.
As the wild beast flees from the elements into the cavern
where his wild dam littered him, so I fled the darkness of my clay.

And naught did I find but the turbulence of my imagination.
There in chaotic pattern did I find the seeds
of all confusion that pretended to be wisdom.

Where man was born was also born his gods.
Where man was born was also born his demons.
And where in glorious pain, man first raised his fetal head,
there too in ignominious joy was he devoured.

My eyes are extinguished although I see the earth beneath me.
My ears are destroyed and my mouth speaks no words,
for my feet carry me through a realm that needs no language.

My mind is silent and humble in its dismay,
and within that House there is not one thought.
And within that House is heard
the painful tolling of a tiny silver bell,
and within that dome is felt the surge of mighty roaring tides
that will not be stopped.

For the keeper of the House is gone,
and all that remains testifies that he never was.
Exploding thunder shakes its walls,
and heaven and hell are within its region.

For All is within that House, swelling it to burst its comprehension.
All joy is here. All joy is pain,
torturing the House that cannot contain it.

All joy is tears, and the world will not contain
the reaving sorrow of this House.
All this House is fire,
straining to burst forth until these walls no longer stand.

O lamentations of lamentations, has thy agony no tongue?
O sorrower in the spaces of desolation, who shall hear thy anguish,
and unless it be heard, how shall the pain be stopped?

I, O Eternal Essence, beseech Thee —
where within Thee have I dissolved myself?

Where are prisoned those who follow love?
Where have I left my I-ness, and now having left it,
who is it that cries out to Thee?

Where is the dirge of sorrow that is all that remains of me?
Who feels this pain that burns and consumes,
yet is felt not by I-who-am-no-more?

Who is it that looks from the windows of my mansion
like a strange prowler? Who is it that hears and hears not,
that yearns for life and lives not, that seeks out death and dies not...?

O Ever-Allness, what is Thy pleasure in my sorrow?
Thou hast damned me to thoughtlessness,
yet I cannot leave off thinking,
and still my thoughts are not words.

Thou hast robbed me of my soul and mind,
and my body laments for all ages,
for my body dies not, nor yet walks among men.
Thou hast delivered me from my Ego and what is there that remains?

O Ever-Allness, forever insensate,
pitiless to entreaty, speechless to my prayers —
weep Thou with me for I am of Thee...
and all that remains of me is Thee.

What is the magnitude of Thy nothingness!
What are the limits of Thy plentitude!
What is the thunder of Thy silence!
How quiet are Thy cataclysms!
Thus shall I sing the praises of myself.

Peace to the wanderer!

Book II

Who shall hear of Moses, Gotama, or Amenhotep, if hearing is not?
Although Jesus weep and Socrates drown,
who shall hear their anguish if there is not hearing?

Who shall know of love and godliness, of peace and serenity,
if knowledge is not?
Who shall not perish in the heavy seas of forgetfulness
if knowledge is not...?
Though his convulsions and agony for life be mountainous—
shall he not perish?

Though the worlds scream from their vertiginous orbits,
how can they cast themselves down while knowing is not...?
Though the stars roar in anguish at their distances,
who shall know of their roaring?

How shall the atom know of the sea...?
How shall the atom know of the universe...?

How shall the spaces know of their nothingness...?
How shall nothingness hear the agony of nature
that cries out against it?

Where, where is where?
Why, why is why?
Where O wise among wise, is when...?
In what drifting sand heaps are its footprints...?
In what continuum is etched its lightning rate
like music etched on ice?

Who, who is who?
Can the sage, more the fool, say that which is being...
and among beings, who are what?
Is the spark an entity, or is it merely part of the flame,
and is the flame only illusory heat, or does it live?

Is not man a question asking questions,
frustrated by the unanswered, laboring to answer himself,
and creating a mountain of questions in the answer...?
Yet who shall know?

Who shall know the circle that has no radius...?
Who shall know the point that is a line of infinity...?

Where is Maya?
If all is Maya, who, knowing, sees this illusion...?
Is not his knowing also Maya?

In what pitiful hells are the wise...?
In what blackest abysses are the oblivious and ignorant...?

How shrill is the hunger of inertia,
how maddening the stupor of extinction that comes from action?

O wise and foolish, look about you in your joys.
Where are the joys of yesterday?
And being gone, did they ever live?
Did you enjoy, or was it another's lips that drained thy cup?

Hear the voice of shadows...
Look about you into the invisible memories of the ether.
Where are they, these joys...?

What matters it if the infant starves,
if the angel is raped,
if the saint burns upon the spit?
Are they not gone? Is the sorrow not gone?
And who shall remember, since knowing is not...?
Who shall hear their anguish?

Where are the beautiful?
Where is their beauty washed by the years...?
Where are the years drowned in the ocean of the Unknowing?

Think ye on the folly of light.
Does it not perish when the eyes are closed?
But the power over us by light is feared by man.
He sleeps and dreams of darkness, and wakens, screaming into it….

Relax ye and die. Live the darkness.
Enter the impassive pool of the Unknowing….

Who shall extol the memory of man,
which leaves him often before his life…?
Who remembers after life?

If man forgets his infancy before his manhood is upon him —
what shall he remember hence…?
Shall he remember nothingness?
Desist and enter the pool of the Unknowing….

What is time, O mind…?
Is it the number of steps in a day, the number of thoughts in a step?
Then, of the thoughts in a day, how many years of days
would it take to know all there is to know…?
Then how long to know the magnitude of the Unknowing…?
How many steps will take thee from here to there?
Who shall anoint thy limbs?

Though he who forgets more
seems greater than he who strived not and died in ignorance…
who shall know…? Who shall know?

Mourn ye for the hour when the cloud of the Unknowing passes
and the falseness of light dazzles the eye.
For the light is a liar unto the Light,
and the light is the darkness of the mind.
Yet who shall know…?

I is dead. Death is dead and life has no living…
All that remains is All.

I of the cloudier corpus is slain.
It is slain that the "I" of the mind might live.

"I" of the mind is slain, for the "I" of the spirit to live.
"I" of the spirit is slain that the spirit may come into its glory.

"I" of the spirit shrinks from the vanity of life. Space is upon it.
Space towers above it, silently mocking its absence.
And the spirit takes its leave like a thought...
like the vapors... like the solitary sound that is heard not....

Eternity wanders through infinity like a blind minnow
in an empty ocean whose bounds are limitless...
Yet who can see its boundlessness?

Eternity probes itself like a blind idiot,
for it know not its immensity,
and it roars and rages in its madness because it cannot find its edges.
Yet who can hear its roaring...?

The candles of time are lit, and their wax congeals in cold spheres....
But they burn so long and die so quickly,
no man knows if they burn.

Eternity convulses in its pralaya, seeking definition.
Death agonizes silently for motion...
All that remains is All.

O who shall hear of this anguish?
All that remains is All.

Book III

O Dream of Dreams, tell me, where is the dreamer?

O Dream of Dreams of Dreams, tell me, where is the dreamer?

O Dreamer, speak unto me — in which of these dreams
wilt thou be found?

O Dreamer, speak unto me. Art thou the dreamer in the Dream,
or the dreamer of the Dream?

O Dreamer, answer me — if thou speakest unto thyself,
and hear the sound of thy voice and reply unto it —
are there then two people speaking, or is it but one?

O Dreamer answer me — how many people are dreaming thy dream?

O eternal spaces, art thou black or white…?
Is thy form clothed in light or darkness?

Reply unto me who walketh in wakefulness,
knowing not if wakefulness be but an illusion of wakefulness,
or if sleep be the door of the Absolute…
Or if sleep be the dreamer awake….

Speak to me, not in the ringing of my ears,
which know not if such stridency be the dawning of new perception,
or the damnation of all that was real.

O world, where are thou, that but a second past clung to my feet?
Where in space am I caught?

O love, where are thy children — the friends of my youth?
Who has frozen them in eternal ice
until they stand in transient memory, seeming as statues…?

Who has placed the halter of time upon their necks,
to swing them in the listless abysses of silence…?

O never-never-forever… Why art Thou?
O tender I-ness forgive me… O lovable I-ness forgive me…
for my hand has shattered the mirror, and I can see thee not.

O hunger that begets creation…
O wistful memory of myself…
O transient I-ness, forgive me,
for the probing finger has shattered the veil of illusion.
I have shattered the chimera of all Knowing…
And all that I know is naught.

Time did I seize in the fingers of my mind,
and that which seemed to move as a phantom
did I hold in my fingers….

The peoples of the earth did I see —,
all that had lived or will live —
and their thoughts were upon their faces.

Beneath my feet did I seize space,
and that which seemed afar was near.
And beneath my feet I suppressed the mountains…
Yet the cool oceans did rise harmlessly to my nostrils.

And in all this land there was not one sound,
for my fingers held all time,
and in time are the fields of motion.
So that no atom stirred, nor did one audible wave afflict the ether.

For the blood of the serpent is coagulated.
In its mind all thoughts are one.

And I saw the voices of men…
And I saw the beautiful patterns of motion…
But the world was as still as death.

And I saw the beauty as it liveth…
yet no color was upon the eye.
The rose upon the bush was only a pale weed,
yet Red and Pink shook the shimmering twilight with loveliness.

And the soft perfume of memory tinted the Void with its essence.
And I saw the flight of the swallow,
rolling across dimension like a silent surf.

And as I looked, I saw the emerald dye of the deep,
drawn from the ocean's waves…
And even the whiteness melted before the snow on the mountaintop.

Plain was the picture. Plain was the picture for I had concentrated
upon color and motion… and now they were no more.

Strange was the land for I concentrated upon dimension
until it waxed and waned, until that which seemed small
was as great as that which seemed great.

The nightingale sang in the gloaming…
His beak is now silent… and yet his song liveth forever.

O friend of my childhood, O lovable I-ness,
what have I done to my world?
I have turned my eye upon it and delivered it unto chaos!

And now I look upon the looker…
Twice I see myself and then I see myself no more.

I see myself as a suppressor of mountainous space
and a conqueror of time.
Mighty are my sinews as I stand upon the mountain.

Then I see myself as an infinitesimal man
in the infinitude of humanity…
caught in the congealed blood of life.

I see this tiny man, happy, living,
responding to illusions of color and motion and dimension,
happy in his response,
not knowing the illusion of his indulgence in non-existent happiness.

And looking upon the tiny man, I see his joys leave him,
for joy is a thing apart.

And looking upon him I see his response leave him,
for motion is a thing apart.

And seeing these things my heart burns with love for existence.
Yes, I on the mountain, conqueror of illusion,
now weep for the beauty of illusion.

And looking back into the panorama below,
I, the mountained man — I the consciousness absolute —
see that the tiny man now no longer lives...
for life is a thing apart.

And since he no longer lives, he cannot see me as I see him,
nor can he see himself as I see him,
nor can he ever know of his joys, which are things apart...
or know of his love, which is now a thing apart.

And knowing his love and his longing for the pattern,
I on the mountain bewail and sorrow in his loss.

Great is my anguish in his silence.
Great is my agony in his loss.
And feeling my agony, I on the mountain,
know that I am the tiny man in the endless cavalcade.

And soon I see, looking ahead, that all my joys are not,
that all my love is not, that all my being is not.
And I see that all Knowing is not.

And the eminent I-ness melts into the embraces of oblivion—
melts into the embraces of oblivion like a charmed lover,
fighting the spell and languishing into it.

And now I breathe Space and walk in Emptiness.
My soul freezes in the void and my thoughts melt
into an indestructible blackness.

My consciousness struggles voiceless to articulate
and screams into the abysses of itself. Yet there is no echo.

All that remains is All.

My spark of life falls through the canyons of the universe
and my soul cannot weep for its loss...
for lamentation and sorrow are things apart.

All that remains is All.

The universe passes like a fitful vision....
The darkness and the void are part of the Unknowing....
Death shall exist forever....
Nothingness is Everywhere....
Silence is forgotten....

All that remains is ALL.

Oxherding Picture Nine: Reaching the Source

Too many steps have been taken returning to the root and the source.
Better to have been blind and deaf from the beginning!
Dwelling in one's true abode, unconcerned with that without --
the river flows tranquilly on and the flowers are red.

From the beginning, truth is clear.
Poised in silence, I observe the forms of integration and disintegration.
One who is not attached to form need not be "reformed."
The water is emerald. The mountain is indigo.
I see that which is creating and that which is destroying.

Oxherding Picture Ten: Return to Society

I mingle with the people of the world.
My clothes are ragged and dust-laden, and I am ever blissful.
I use no magic to extend my life.
Now, before me, the dead trees become alive.

Inside my gate, a thousand sages do not know me.
The beauty of my garden is invisible.
Why should one search for the footprints of the patriarchs?
I enter the market place with few possessions on my staff.
Everyone I look upon is enlightened.

Avadhuta Gita
Song of the Ever-Free

Dattatreya

The *Avadhuta Gita* is a Hindu text expounding on the non-dual philosophy of Advaita Vedanta. Authorship is attributed to Dattatreya, who some say was the teacher of Patanjali, but no historical data exists about when or where he was born or how long he lived.

The word *Avadhuta* means a liberated soul, one who has "shaken off" all worldly attachments and cares, and has attained a state of God-realization. An Avadhuta feels no need of observing any rules, either secular or religious. He seeks nothing, avoids nothing, and claims neither knowledge nor ignorance. The Avadhuta has done away with worldly concerns and standard social etiquette, at least in his or her heart. As such, they are said to be "free to roam the earth as a child."

According to Dattatreya, the free man, the Avadhuta, need not have any particular appearance, lifestyle, religion or social role. He may walk about naked or be dressed as a prince. He may appear pious or blasphemous, ascetic or hedonistic.

Swami Vivekananda, a great Advaita teacher, often quoted from the *Avadhuta Gita*. He once said, "Men like the one who wrote this Song have deeply realized. They care for nothing, feel nothing done to the body, care not for heat, cold, danger, or anything. They sit still, enjoying the bliss of Atman, and though red-hot coals burn the body, they feel them not."

1. Self

By the grace of God the Absolute,
the desire to realize one's natural state of Unity
arises in the wisest of men,
and provides them refuge from all fear.

    1.1

All that appears in the realm of forms is Self and Self alone —
the One Being, the never-dying Source of Bliss.
How can I worship that which is formless, limitless,
and incapable of separation?

    1.2

This universe composed of the five elements —
space, air, fire, water and earth —
is only the shimmering of a mirage within me,
the immaculate One. To whom shall I bow?

    1.3

All is Self. There is neither separation nor wholeness.
How can I say, "This exists," or "That does not exist"?
I am awestruck by this Great Mystery!

    1.4

The essence and totality of Vedanta is this:
I am the formless, all-pervading Self — the Absolute.
Realization of This is Intelligence.

    1.5

I am God, the Self of All. Of this there is no doubt.
My nature is boundless, changeless, indivisible like sky —
purity itself, untouched by illusion.
Truly, truly, I am That.

    1.6

Indeed, my nature is pure Intelligence.
I am infinite, immutable, deathless.
I experience neither joy or sorrow,
nor do I know to whom these might appear to exist.

    1.7

In me there is no act of mind, good or bad.
In me there is no act of body, good or bad.
In me there is no act of speech, good or bad.
I am pure transcendent Consciousness, beyond the senses.

    1.8

The mind is like space. It seems to face in all directions.   1.9
It seems to imply a past. It seems to encompass all.
But in Reality, it has no substance and cannot be said to exist.

I am Self, the One and only, untouched by space and time.   1.10
How can it be said that Self is or is not?
I am existence itself, both manifest and unmanifest.
I am both visible and hidden.

Do you not yet understand that it is you who are the Self?   1.11
You are the eternal, self-reflecting Lord of all that is and is not,
the ever-shining, ever-exalted Atman.
How can you continue to grieve day and night?

I abide as Self Alone, the Absolute, the all-pervasive One.   1.12
I am both perceiver and that which is perceived.
The indivisible cannot be divided.

You were never born, nor can you ever die.   1.13
At no time have you ever had a body.
The scriptures teach this well-known truth in many
different ways: "All is Brahman."

You are That for which inside and outside have no meaning.   1.14
You are the Absolute, existing everywhere at once and forever.
Why do you run here and there like a hungry ghost?

Separateness and Oneness do not exist for "you" and "me."   1.15
There is no you. There is no me. There is no universe.
All is Self and Self alone.

The world and body depicted by the senses is not you.   1.16
Nor do the world and body belong to you,
nor do you belong to the body and world.
You are the Supreme Self in which bodies and worlds arise.
Why do you grieve in the body?
Why do you suffer in the world?

For you there is no birth or death.   1.17
For you there is no mind or memory, no good or bad.
For you there is no bondage or liberation.
O dear child, why the tears?
You and I have no form. You and I have no name.

Dear child, why do you roam the world like a ghost?   1.18
Behold! You are Self—that which cannot be divided.
Do not crave the world. Be happy!

You are Truth. You do not move. You do not change.   1.19
You are the ever-free, the unshakable One.
In you there is neither attachment nor aversion.
Why do you seek objects of desire and cause yourself to suffer?

The scriptures all say that Self is without attributes or qualities,   1.20
that Self is clear, deathless, and without a body,
that Self exists everywhere at once, and nowhere.
Know that I am That. Know that you are That.
Never doubt it!

That which has form is not real.   1.21
That in which forms arise is eternal.
Realizing this, you are no longer subject to birth and death.

Sages sometimes call Self the "ever-same."   1.22
Let go of attachments and the ever–many mind will forget itself.

If your nature is not-Self, how can there be Self-Realization?   1.23
If your nature is Self, how can there be Self-Realization?
If your nature is both Self and not-Self,
how can there be Self-Realization?
If Self alone Is, what is there to realize?

You are the pure, unchanging essence of existence,   1.24
free of form and death. How can you know or not know God?

It is of Self, the Absolute, that the scriptures say,   1.25
"I am Brahman," and "Thou art That."
Of the ego and the phenomenal world,
the scriptures say, "Not this, not this…"

Self contains universe. Self contains mind. Self contains "you."   1.26
There is no one to stand apart and contemplate Self.
There is no mechanism for contemplation.
There is nothing to contemplate.
Why do you so shamelessly think otherwise?

The Absolute cannot be known.   1.27
How can I speak of the Absolute?
God cannot be known. How can I worship God?
I am One with no other, the only Truth, the single essence.
I am eternal, formless, solitary, endless.
Who is there to speak about and worship This?

The ego-sense is not the Truth.   1.28
I am not bound by the twenty-four cosmic principles.
I am neither the perceiver nor that which is perceived.
I am the singular Reality beyond all that,
beyond the furthest reaches of imagination.
How then could I know my own nature? Can the eye see itself?

That which appears to have form and substance   1.29
cannot by its very nature be infinite or immortal,
nor can it even be said to be "real" while it lasts.
Self alone is Reality. It does not kill, nor can it be killed.

You are the pure, formless, ever-same Reality.   1.30
You have no beginning or end.
How can you be confused about Self?
How can you hold on to delusions about True Nature?

When a jar is broken, the jar-space it defined   1.31
is not different from infinite boundless space.
Like this, when the ego-mind lets go,
that which you are is not different from the immaculate Self.

In Reality, there is no jar nor interior jar-space.
Neither is there an individual self nor an individual soul.
Realize that in Brahman, the Absolute,
there is no knower, no knowledge, no capacity to know.
In Brahman there is nothing to be known. — 1.32

Realize I am That which is always and everywhere.
I am Void and that which appears in Void.
I am eternal unchanging All. Do not doubt this. — 1.33

There are no scriptures, no worlds, no people, no religions,
no gods, no sacrificial rites. There are no castes, no races,
no births, no deaths, no lineages or stages of life.
There is neither the path of smoke nor the path of light.
Only the ever-same Brahman, the highest Truth,
the Supreme Reality exists. — 1.34

You are One without other,
free of both the pervaded and the pervader.
Do you believe you are perceptible by the senses?
Do you believe you are beyond the range of senses? — 1.35

Some seek Unity. Most seek duality. Neither realize Truth.
Truth is the same at all times everywhere.
Truth knows nothing of one-ness or two-ness. — 1.36

Truth cannot be described.
Truth is beyond mind and words.
Truth is void of colors and is not white.
Truth is void of sound and all other attributes.
Truth is inaccessible to thought and speech. — 1.37

When you realize that the body, the world,
and all other appearances are unreal and empty like sky,
then you become Brahman.
The paradigm of duality no longer applies to you. — 1.38

Personal self and Supreme Self are not different to me.
All is emptiness, like space.
How can there be an observer of this? — 1.39

What I do, what I eat, what I give, what I give up —
none of this is mine in any way.
I am clear, untouchable, forever unborn and deathless.

Realize these truths:
The universe is formless and without substance.
The universe never changes.
The universe is existence itself, pure and undifferentiated.
The nature of the universe is the Absolute.

Truly, you are Self, the Absolute. There is no doubt about this.
What more do I know? Self is imperceptible to itself,
but it is not imperceptible. If you do not see every being
and all things as Self, you are still ignorant.

Dear child, how can there be illusion or absence of illusion?
How can there be shadow and lack of shadow?
All is one Truth. All is unstained emptiness, like space.

I am forever free and boundless,
no beginning, no middle, no end.
My nature is pure and spotless.
This is my sure knowledge.

This whole grand universe, beginning with the idea
of cosmic intelligence, appears as nothing to me.
Truly, all is Brahman.
How can there be an identity or stages of life?

There is only one indivisible Reality, and I am That.
I know This in every way.
The void, the universe, and the five elements —
space, air, energy, water and earth — in Reality do not exist.

Self is neither eunuch, man nor woman.
Self is not ignorance, knowledge or imagination.
Why do you ponder whether Self is bliss or absence of bliss?

Self is not realized through the practice of yoga.   1.48
Self is not realized by destroying the mind.
Self is not realized by instructions from teachers.
There is nothing for Self to realize.
It is Truth itself.
It is itself the Illumined One.

There is no body created by the five elements,   1.49
nor is there a state of disembodiment.
All is Self and Self alone. How can the three states
of waking, dreaming and deep sleep be ascribed to Self?
If the three states are false, how can there be a fourth state?

I am eternal, free, unbound. From what could I be liberated?   1.50
I am not separate from Brahman.
I am neither the doer nor the experiencer.
I see no difference between the pervader and the pervaded.

Just as water poured into water   1.51
becomes water without distinction,
so the universe and True Nature are One to me.

Self is never bound nor liberated.   1.52
Do you think Self must either be constrained
or free from constraint?

Your True Nature is empty and all-pervasive, like sky.   1.53
Your body and all visible things are like water in a mirage.

I have no teacher. I have no teachings.   1.54
I have no disciples or duties, no attributes or actions.
My nature is pure, incorporeal and clear, like space.

You have no body. You have no mind. You are purity itself.   1.55
Do not be afraid to say, "I am God."

O mind, why do you grieve?   1.56
Truly, you are Self. Never doubt This.
Drink, my child, the nectar of the ocean of Oneness.

There is neither knowledge nor ignorance,   1.57
nor is there some combination of knowledge and ignorance.
One who realizes This becomes pure Intelligence,
and is forever Home.

I have no need for knowledge and reasoning,   1.58
no need for concepts like time and space,
no need for instruction from teachers,
no need for attaining Samadhi.
I am Truth itself, the one Reality.
My nature is clear and empty, like sky.

I was not born and I will never die.   1.59
I perform no actions, good or bad.
I am pure Brahman, without qualities or attributes.
Bondage and liberation have no meaning.

God is unchanging, complete, undivided. God pervades All.   1.60
How can you be inside or outside of God?

This whole grand Universe of the Absolute shines forth,   1.61
undivided, unbounded, unchanging.
The concept of illusion is also illusion.
Duality and non-duality exist only in imagination.

To both the manifest world and unmanifest potential,   1.62
say, "Not this, not this…"
The Absolute alone exists, free of separation and oneness.

You have no mother, no father, no spouse, no children,   1.63
no kinsmen, no acquaintances, no friends.
You are neither attached to, nor unattached from, anything.
O mind, why do you suffer so?

O mind, there is no day or night, no rising and setting of suns.   1.64
O wise one, why do you imagine forms in formlessness?

Self is neither whole nor divided.   1.65
Self experiences neither joy nor grief.
Self is and is not everything and nothing.

I am neither the performer nor the witness.   1.66
I have no works, no actions, no karma—now or formerly.
I have no body, nor am I disembodied.
How can anything be "mine" or "not mine"?

I have no faults, like passion and attachment.   1.67
There is no pain of a body, or pain anywhere for me.
I know only This.
I am the One Self, vast and stainless as sky.

O mind, what use is your vain talk?   1.68
Everything you see is only conjecture.
I have made known to you the essence of Reality.
You are Truth itself, boundless and clear as space.

In whatever place or manner, or in whatever state a yogi dies,   1.69
he is absorbed into the Absolute,
just as the jar-space of a broken jar
is absorbed into limitless space.

Whether he quits the body in a holy shrine   1.70
or in the house of an untouchable, the realized yogi—
even if his body is in a coma—becomes the Absolute, Brahman.

The realized yogi knows everything in life—duty, wealth,   1.71
family, enjoyment, freedom, desire, and all the stationary
and movable things of the world, like trees and men—
to be without substance, and as unreal as water in a mirage.

I perform no actions, nor do I witness activity.   1.72
There is no past in which I performed actions
or witnessed activity. There is no future
in which I will perform actions or witness activity.
I know this beyond a shadow of a doubt.

The Avadhuta abides alone in a quiet place,   1.73
absorbed in the perfection of Brahman.
Having transcended ego and pride, he roams about naked,
breathing the mystery of All as Self.

Where there exists neither the three states of consciousness,   1.74
nor a forth state of transcendence — there one becomes Atman.
Where there is neither freedom nor bondage,
neither good nor bad, how can desire exist?

One does not become Brahman by reciting scriptures,   1.75
repeating mantras, or practicing tantric rites.
This is the true and faithful utterance of the Avadhuta,
purified by no-thought and absorbed in the Oneness of Being.

All is both void and full, everything and nothing.   1.76
In Brahman neither truths nor untruths exist.
The Avadhuta sings this Gita spontaneously,
from his personal experience and his knowledge of scriptures.

Chapter 2

When looking for a true teacher, do not be concerned   2.1
if he is young and addicted to sensual pleasure.
Do not be concerned if he is illiterate, a servant,
or a householder. None of these things matter.
Would you cast aside a diamond because of dust?

Do not consider scholarship to be the test of a teacher.   2.2
It matters little whether or not a guru can recite scriptures.
The wise ones feel his essence. A boat does not need beauty
or vermillion paint to ferry you across.

Without effort, the Supreme One encompasses   2.3
both the movable and the unchanging,
the manifest and the unmanifest.
It is Awareness itself, still and transparent as sky.

Without effort, the Supreme One appears   2.4
as living and inert, animate and inanimate.
How can you talk about it being this or that?
It is all things at all times all at once.

I am more subtle than primordial substance,   2.5
more primal than elements, essences and compounds.
I am prior to notions of birth and death.
I am still, undivided, indifferent.

It is said my all-pervading formlessness   2.6
is worshipped by the gods.
In undivided emptiness, there is no difference between gods,
nor between gods and not-gods.

Illusory life does not make me doubt.   2.7
Movements of mind do not touch me.
Thoughts and volitions arise in me like bubbles in a river,
then vanish into the pool of Unknowing.

As the qualities of softness and hardness,
sweetness and bitterness, are inseparable
from their respective objects, so do I pervade all existence
and non-existence.

2.8

As the softness, coldness or sweetness of water
is not separate from the water,
so are worldly existence and the Absolute inseparable to me.

2.9

The Lord of the Universe is unnamable.
His subtlety is more subtle than the subtlest.
He is spotless, beyond the senses, beyond mind and intellect.
He is Supreme.

2.10

Knowing the nature of Being to be indivisible and unchanging,
how can you believe there's an "I"?
How can there be a "you" or "me"?
How can there be a world?

2.11

True Nature is like space — truly like space.
Infinite, clear, empty, blameless, full.

2.12

Brahman walks not the Earth.
It is neither carried by wind nor submerged in water.
It does not dwell in fire.

2.13

Brahman pervades all Space. Nothing pervades Brahman.
Brahman exists both inside and outside itself.
Brahman is complete, undivided, uninterrupted.

2.14

Brahman is subtle, invisible, without qualities.
Realization of Brahman does not come on first hearing.
Realization comes with practice.

2.15

Realization comes through faithful practice of yoga.
When consciousness abides with no object, dissolution happens.
The realized yogi becomes the Absolute.
His faults and merits are absorbed into All.

2.16

There is only one antidote to the poison of worldly illusion—
the sweetness of True Nature.

2.17

Forms are visible to the eye.
The formless is imagined in mind.
Brahman is neither. It is beyond existence and non-existence.
Sometimes it is called Inner Self.

2.18

Maya and *prakriti* create and experience the illusory universe.
The offerings of experience can be compared to a coconut.
The outer layer is the husk. Within the husk is the pith,
within the pith, the shell, within the shell,
the kernel of dense white flesh.
Seek to know that which is inside the kernel of flesh.
Drink the milk of Brahma.

2.19

Knowledge of outer appearances is false knowledge,
pertaining only to an ephemeral illusion.
Knowledge of inner truths and explanations
is a step away from ignorance, but knowing Brahma
is the only wisdom. Brahma is the milk of the coconut.

2.20

On a full-moon night, you see one clear and brilliant moon.
See Self like this, transparent, luminous, singular.
There is only one moon, only One Self.
Duality is an error of vision.

2.21

All perceived distinctions are defects of your own seeing,
not valid attributes of the all-pervading One.
One who realizes Truth becomes Brahman.
One who teaches Truth, is worthy of the highest praise.

2.22

Whether he is illiterate or learned, whoever comes
to full awareness of Truth by the grace of the Guru within,
is no longer fooled by the mirage of world.

2.23

He who is free from animosity and attachment,
whose commitment and effort never waver,
who works for the welfare of all beings—
such a one shall realize God.

2.24

As when a jar breaks, the jar-space it defines   2.25
becomes one with infinite Space,
so when a yogi quits his body, the ego-self it formed
becomes infinite Self — the One Awareness.

It has been said that one's final deathbed desire   2.26
determines one's next birth.
This applies only to those who live lives of worldly action.
It does not apply to realized yogis.

The destiny of those living lives of worldly action   2.27
can be expressed in speech.
The destiny of yogis transcends expression.

Yogis follow no particular path.   2.28
They surrender self and attainment happens.

No matter where a yogi dies —   2.29
whether in a holy place or the house of an untouchable —
he becomes Supreme Self alone,
and never again enters a womb.

One who realizes Supreme Self,   2.30
which is innate, inconceivable and unborn,
is not tainted by fulfillment of desires, nor defiled by any evil.
He performs no actions and is not bound by karma.
He is forever free and benevolent to all.
He lives as he likes and accumulates no stain.

One who realizes Supreme Self, which is formless and eternal,   2.31
is beyond the realm of opposites. He lives on with no body,
no desire, no fear, no hope, no support.
Not bound by illusion, his power is without limit or end.

One who realizes Supreme Self finds no scriptures,   2.32
no teachers, no students, no initiations, no shaved heads,
no postures, no meditation or anything else.

One who realizes Supreme Self
finds no *sambhavi, sakti,* or *anavi* initiations.
He finds no sphere of flesh, no images or symbols,
no hands, no feet, no jars or any other thing
with a beginning, middle and end.

2.33

One who realizes Supreme Self becomes
that from which the universe emerges,
that by which the universe is maintained,
and that into which the universe is dissolved.
In the still water of Self, bubbles of universe arise,
linger and disappear.

2.34

One who realizes Supreme Self has no use for yoga postures,
fixed gazing, control of breath, or exercise of the nerve-current.
Attainment and non-attainment are meaningless to him.

2.35

One who realizes Supreme Self is devoid of all relative notions,
like one and many, great and small, full and empty,
all and nothing, same and different. He is devoid of notions
about knowledge, knower and knowableness,
of ideas about capacity and measurement,
of concepts like equality and disparity.

2.36

One who realizes Supreme Self does so regardless of being
disciplined or undisciplined, wealthy or impoverished,
active or withdrawn, sensual or restrained.

2.37

One who realizes Supreme Self
knows beyond a shadow of doubt that he is not the body,
not the mind, not the senses, not the ego, not intelligence,
that he is neither the subtle elements nor the gross elements,
nor is his nature that of space.

2.38

One who realizes Supreme Self transcends the injunctions
of scriptures. He claims neither purity nor impurity.
He admits no duty or absence of duty.
Notions of separation and oneness do not apply to him.
Even that which the scriptures prohibit for others,
for him is permissible.

2.39

How can the guru teach that which cannot be grasped
by mind or expressed in speech?
Through the teacher who is ever-one with Brahma,
the light of Truth shines without words.

Chapter 3

How can one worship Shiva the Absolute,
which is neither personal nor impersonal,
which is both omni-formed and formless,
which is beyond love and hate, merit and fault,
passion and dispassion, attachment and non-attachment?
Shiva has no attributes to worship.
Nor are there attributes it lacks.

3.1

Shiva the Absolute is devoid of colors and is not white.
It recognizes no diversity and harbors no doubt.
It is not bound by cause and effect,
nor is it subject to imagination.
O dear friend, I am Shiva the Absolute!
Who is there to bow to solitary Self?

3.2

I am not the origin, nor am I the originator.
I am the ever-shining sun, that which never is not.
I am not clouded nor clear, bright nor dark, rooted nor rootless.
I am the ever-shining sun, that which never is not.
I am Love-Truth-Awareness, boundless as sky.

3.3

How can I say the indifferent One has desires?
How can I say the ever-free Self has attachments?
How can I say the void Absolute has substance?
How can I say the perceivable All does or does not have reality?
I am Love-Truth-Awareness, boundless as sky.

3.4

How can I describe That which is beyond duality
and non-duality? What is there to talk about?
How can I say That which is beyond existence
and non-existence is or is not eternal?
All is Unknowing. All is Mystery.
I am Love-Truth-Awareness, boundless as sky.

3.5

Atman is neither gross nor subtle. It has no highs or lows.
Atman neither appears nor disappears. It has no beginning,
no middle, no end. This is the Absolute Truth of Reality.
I am Love-Truth-Awareness, boundless as sky.

3.6

Realize that sense-objects are without substance, like space.
So are the sense organs that perceive them.
Realize that Atman is beyond the bondage of appearances,
beyond even liberation from it. Never doubt this.
I am Love-Truth-Awareness, boundless as sky.

3.7

Dear one, I am not hidden or difficult to comprehend.
I am not inscrutable or inaccessible.
I am Here, available for Seeing!
I am Love-Truth-Awareness, boundless as sky.

3.8

I have no karma. I am the fire in which all karma is consumed.
I have no sorrow. I am the fire in which all sorrow is consumed.
I have no body. I am the fire in which all bodies —
gross, subtle and causal — are consumed.
I am Love-Truth-Awareness, boundless as sky.

3.9

I have no sin. I am the fire that burns the sins of the sinless.
I have no attributes. I am the fire in which attributes disappear.
I have no limitations.
I am the fire in which bondage and freedom evaporate.
I am Love-Truth-Awareness, boundless as sky.

3.10

Dear one, mind is not absent from me,
nor can I be said to have mind.
I am not devoid of thoughts and feelings,
nor can I be said to have them.
I am not separate from existence, nor can I be said to exist.
I am Love-Truth-Awareness, boundless as sky.

3.11

I am beyond illusion. I cannot even imagine a state of delusion.
I am beyond joy and sorrow. I do not know them at all.
I have no desire or greed. There I nothing I lack or want.
I am Love-Truth-Awareness, boundless as sky.

3.12

The creeper vine of worldly life does not entangle me.   3.13
The vast array of pleasures and contentments do not tempt me.
The bondage of ignorance does not ensnare me.
I am Love-Truth-Awareness, boundless as sky.

The entire expanse of worldly passions causes no ripple in Me.   3.14
The entire expanse of worldly sorrows causes no ripple in Me.
The entire expanse of worldly goodness causes no ripple in Me.
I am Love-Truth-Awareness, boundless as sky.

I am not the source of actions resulting in misery and regret,   3.15
nor am I the ego-mind that suffers misery and regret.
Even that which causes the ego-mind to arise is not me.
I am Love-Truth-Awareness, boundless as sky.

I am the death of movement in the unmoving One.   3.16
I neither think nor decide, nor am I indecisive.
I am the death of sleep and wakefulness. I am neither
good nor evil, moving nor still, substantial nor ephemeral.
I am Love-Truth-Awareness, boundless as sky.

I cannot be known, nor can I know.   3.17
I am not the way of knowing.
I am invisible to the mind,
imperceptible to the senses,
unapproachable through words.
How can I transmit This to you?
I am Love-Truth-Awareness, boundless as sky.

I am the Supreme Reality, forever whole and undivided.   3.18
I have no inside or outside, nor any other imaginings of duality.
Before anything was, I Am. I never am not.
I am Love-Truth-Awareness, boundless as sky.

I am the Supreme Reality, devoid of passion, jealousy,   3.19
hatred and all other trappings of body, mind and gods.
Though I contain the miseries and sufferings
of the imaginary world, I am not touched by them.
I am Love-Truth-Awareness, boundless as sky.

I am the Supreme Reality.   3.20
In a realm where the three states of consciousness do not apply,
how can there be a fourth state of transcendence?
In a realm with no center or edges,
how can there be up or down, north or south, east or west?
In a realm without beginning, middle or end,
how can there be past, present or future?
I am Love-Truth-Awareness, boundless as sky.

In Self, there are no divisions or separate objects,   3.21
neither massive or minute. There is no difference between
long and short, wide and narrow, angular or round.
I am Love-Truth-Awareness, boundless as sky.

I have no father, no mother, no children, no kinsmen.   3.22
I was never born and cannot die. I never had a mind.
I am forever tranquil and untroubled.
I am Love-Truth-Awareness, boundless as sky.

My nature is clear and infinite, beyond ideas of purity and stain.   3.23
I am indefinable, unattached, unknowable.
I am Love-Truth-Awareness, boundless as sky.

If I am the undivided One — and I am —   3.24
how can there be Brahma and all the many gods?
How can there be residents of heaven and earth?
How can there be heaven and earth?
I am Love-Truth-Awareness, boundless as sky.

I am Supreme Reality. How can I say I am "this," or "not this,"   3.25
or neither or both. I am beyond all that.
How can I say I am time-bound or eternal? How can I say
I have a body or do not have a body? I am beyond all that!
I am Love-Truth-Awareness, boundless as sky.

I perform no actions yet my activity is endless.   3.26
I have no attachments yet I love all things.
I have no body yet I enjoy endless pleasure.
I am Love-Truth-Awareness, boundless as sky.

The phenomenal stage-play of Maya does not disturb me.   3.27
Deceit and arrogance do not bother me.
Tyranny and evil do not affect me.
Truth and untruth, to me are the same.
I am Love-Truth-Awareness, boundless as sky.

Divisions of time like morning and twilight do not exist in me.   3.28
I am ever-present, and not contained by time.
I have no knowledge to impart, but I am not deaf or mute.
I am free of ignorance, but know the ways of thought.
I am Love-Truth-Awareness, boundless as sky.

I am not a master nor do I have a master. I am unperplexed.   3.29
I am beyond mind and no-mind, forever undisturbed.
I am beyond all dualities — truly unshakable.
I am Love-Truth-Awareness, boundless as sky.

How can I say, "This is a forest," or "This is a temple"?   3.30
How can I say something is proven or doubtful?
I am motionless, all pervading, indifferent.
I am Love-Truth-Awareness, boundless as sky.

I am not alive, nor am I lifeless.   3.31
Not bound by such dualities, I light eternity.
I have no origin, nor does anything originate from me.
Not bound by such dualities, I light eternity.
I am Love-Truth-Awareness, boundless as sky.

Not bound by birth and death, I light eternity.   3.32
Not trapped in worldly existence, I light eternity.
Not subject to creation and destruction, I light eternity.
I am Love-Truth-Awareness, boundless as sky.

You are Self. You have no name or form,   3.33
nor even an allusion to them.
You are no-thing, and have no substance whatever.
O shameless mind, how can you continually complain?
I am Love-Truth-Awareness, boundless as sky.

Dear heart, why do you weep?   3.34
In you there is no old age and death.
In you there is no birth and misery.
Dear heart, why do you weep?
In you, Changeless One, nothing is never not perfect.
I am Love-Truth-Awareness, boundless as sky.

Dear heart, why do you weep?   3.35
For you there is no form or emptiness.
Dear heart, why do you weep?
For you there is no deformity or beauty,
no aging, no passing of time.
I am Love-Truth-Awareness, boundless as sky.

Dear heart, why do you weep? You have no age.   3.36
Dear heart, why do you weep? You have no mind.
Dear heart, why do you weep? You have no senses.
I am Love-Truth-Awareness, boundless as sky.

Dear heart, why do you weep? You have no lust.   3.37
Dear heart, why do you weep? You have no greed.
Dear heart, why do you weep? You have no delusion.
I am Love-Truth-Awareness, boundless as sky.

Why do you desire wealth? You have no property to secure.   3.38
Why do you desire wealth? You have no wife to support.
Why do you desire wealth? You have no capacity to possess.
I am Love-Truth-Awareness, boundless as sky.

The created world of illusion is not my doing nor yours.   3.39
It belongs to the shameless mind.
There are no different things in That which you truly are.
I am Love-Truth-Awareness, boundless as sky.

In Self there is not one iota of attachment or non-attachment, 3.40
not one iota of passion or dispassion, not one iota of desire.
I am Love-Truth-Awareness, boundless as sky.

In Self there is no observer or observing,　　　　　　　3.41
nor are there objects of observation.
In Self there is no inside or out,
no space, no matter, no time. In Self there is no Samadhi.
I am Love-Truth-Awareness, boundless as sky.

I have conveyed to you the essence of Truth.　　　　　　3.42
There is no you. There is no me.
There is no great being, guru or disciple.
Supreme Reality is astoundingly simple,
and absolutely spontaneous.
I am Love-Truth-Awareness, boundless as sky.

If the Supreme One alone exists, clear and empty like sky,　　3.43
how can there be a higher supreme one?
If it is Ultimate Truth itself that is all-pervading like space,
how can there be a superior ultimate truth?
How can you hope to find it through knowledge and intuition?

Realize undifferentiated Awareness,　　　　　　　　　3.44
which is void of fire, which has not air, earth or water.
Realize undifferentiated Awareness,
which is stiller than still, which is vast and endless as space.

I am not formless, nor do I lack form.　　　　　　　　3.45
I am neither beautiful nor ugly, pure nor impure.
My Nature is mine alone.

Renounce the world! Renounce renunciation!　　　　　　3.46
Renounce non-renunciation! Surrender the poison of ego-ideas
about shunning or accepting Maya.
You are Self — immaculate, immutable, immortal.

Chapter 4

Brahman cannot be invoked or banished.   4.1
Brahman is formless, without source or seed.
What is this offering of flowers and leaves?
What is this meditation and chanting of mantras?
Are you enticing that which is beyond duality and non-duality?

Brahman is not only free of ideas about bondage and liberation,   4.2
free of ideas about immaculateness and stain,
free of ideas about unity and separateness—
Brahman is Ever-Free.

Some say the world is real, others say it has no reality.   4.3
I have no doubts or cares about either.
I am before and beyond such notions—
my nature is Absolute Freedom.

Stainless or stained, divided or whole, different or same...   4.4
I am before and beyond such notions—
my nature is Absolute Freedom.

Concepts like ignorance and intelligence do not occur to me.   4.5
I am never conscious of knowing Self.
How can I say, "I am Awake," or "I am not Awake"?
I am before and beyond such notions—
my nature is Absolute Freedom.

Self is not virtuous or sinful, not bound or free.   4.6
Self is not unity or separateness.
I am before and beyond such notions—
my nature is Absolute Freedom.

I have no friends or enemies. I have no ideas   4.7
about superior and inferior, nor about neutrality.
How can I say, "This is good," or "This is evil"?
I am before and beyond such notions—
my nature is Absolute Freedom.

I am not the object of worship, nor am I the devotee.   4.8
I have no teachings or practices to offer.
What can be said about No-Thing?
I am before and beyond such notions —
my nature is Absolute Freedom.

There is nothing Here that pervades or is pervaded.   4.9
There is nothing Here that is homeless or has a home.
How can I say I am fullness or emptiness?
I am before and beyond such notions —
my nature is Absolute Freedom.

Self has no cause and causes no effect.   4.10
It does not understand and cannot be understood.
How can I speak of it as being perceptible or imperceptible?
I am before and beyond such notions —
my nature is Absolute Freedom.

Self knows nothing and is not knowable.   4.11
Self does not divide or destroy,
nor can Self be divided or destroyed.
Dear child, how can I speak of Self as having a past or future?
I am before and beyond such notions —
my nature is Absolute Freedom.

I have no senses, no mind, no intellect, no knowledge.   4.12
I am neither with or without a body.
How can I speak about desire and dispassion?
I am before and beyond such notions —
my nature is Absolute Freedom.

Self is not separate or superior.   4.13
It is forever whole and equal to itself.
How can I speak about difference and sameness in Brahman?
I am before and beyond such notions —
my nature is Absolute Freedom.

Discipline and self-restraint never occur to me,   4.14
nor do religious austerities and practices.
I have no senses to control or conquer.
How can I speak about triumph and defeat?
I am before and beyond such notions—
my nature is Absolute Freedom.

I have no form, nor am I formless.   4.15
I have no beginning, no duration, no end.
Dear friend, how can I say I am strong or weak?
I am before and beyond such notions—
my nature is Absolute Freedom.

Death and deathlessness, poison and nectar, good and evil—   4.16
dear child, these do not arise in me.
How can I say I am pure or impure?
I am before and beyond such notions—
my nature is Absolute Freedom.

I have never dreamed or awakened.   4.17
I do not meditate, practice devotions, or do yoga postures.
For me there is no day or night, misery or bliss.
How can I speak about deep sleep and transcendence?
I am before and beyond such notions—
my nature is Absolute Freedom.

Know that I am All and I am free of All.   4.18
Know that Maya is not of me, nor is the absence of Maya.
How can I speak about prescribed religious disciplines?
I am before and beyond such notions—
my nature is Absolute Freedom...
I am before and beyond such notions—
my nature is Absolute Freedom.

Know that I am forever Brahman.   4.19
Know that I am forever unbound by concepts
like attainment and failure.
How can I speak about unity and ignorance?
I am before and beyond such notions—
my nature is Absolute Freedom.

I am neither learned nor illiterate,
neither inarticulate nor eloquent.
I am free of silence and the absence of silence.
How can I speak about reason and doubt?
I am before and beyond such notions —
my nature is Absolute Freedom.

4.20

I have no mother, no father, no family, no caste.
I know nothing of birth and death.
How can I speak about affection and loss?
I am before and beyond such notions —
my nature is Absolute Freedom.

4.21

I am the ever-rising sun. Never am I not.
My effulgence is neither light nor dark,
nor the absence of light or darkness.
How can religious devotions apply to me?
I am before and beyond such notions —
my nature is Absolute Freedom.

4.22

Realize for certain that I am without origin.
Realize for certain that I am without division.
Realize for certain that I am without the stain of Maya.
I am before and beyond such notions —
my nature is Absolute Freedom.

4.23

The wise ones give up devotions and practices.
They give up all activity, bad and good,
and drink only the nectar of renunciation.
I am before and beyond such notions —
my nature is Absolute Freedom.

4.24

Where knowing cannot go, how can there be knowledge?
Supremely pure and free, absorbed in infinite bliss,
the Avadhuta spontaneously sings the song of Absolute Reality.

4.25

Chapter 5

The utterance "OM" is pure and all-pervasive like sky,   5.1
free of concepts and connotations. It carries no ideas
of high and low, absolute and relative.
Some say it is the sound of Brahman.
When Brahman is realized as Self, the manifested universe
and the unmanifested void are seen as the same.
What use then is the utterance "OM."

The scriptures have declared, "Thou art That"   5.2
and revealed your true nature is Brahman.
You are devoid of all attributes and obstructions.
You are the same as Everything. You are the only One.
Knowing Self to be All, why does your mind choose to suffer?

You have no height or breadth or depth.   5.3
You have no inside or out. You are without number
but are not the multitudes. To say you are One is one too many.
Knowing Self to be All, why does your mind choose to suffer?

Brahman cannot be realized by following prescribed rules.   5.4
Brahman cannot be realized by performing religious rituals.
Brahman cannot be realized by reasoning or examination.
Brahman cannot be realized by chanting euphonic sounds.
There is no cause and effect between actions and Realization.
Knowing Self to be All, why does your mind choose to suffer?

Samadhi is not the confluence of ego-self and emptiness.   5.5
Samadhi is not the union of consciousness and space.
Samadhi is not the meeting point of time and absence of time.
Knowing Self to be All, why does your mind choose to suffer?

In Brahman, there is no jar, nor is there space inside the jar.   5.6
There is no body, nor is there a soul indwelling the body.
There is no such thing as cause and effect.
Knowing Self to be All, why does your mind choose to suffer?

In the endless freedom of all-pervasive Brahman,
there are no concepts like short and long, round and angular.
Knowing Self to be All, why does your mind choose to suffer?

5.7

Brahman is neither manifest nor void, neither pure nor impure,
neither clear nor the nature of smoke.
Brahman is not everything, not nothing, not either, not both.
Knowing Self to be All, why does your mind choose to suffer?

5.8

In Brahman there is no difference between same and different.
There is no distinction between outside and inside,
nor is there a meeting ground of opposites.
Brahman has no enemies or friends and is equal to All.
Knowing Self to be All, why does your mind choose to suffer?

5.9

In Brahman there are no names like teacher and disciple,
animate and inanimate, living and dead. There is only
unending freedom in the infinite vastness of Self.
Knowing Self to be All, why does your mind choose to suffer?

5.10

Brahman has no form or body, nor is it formless.
Brahman exists without evolution. It never begins nor ends.
In Brahman there is no possibility of separateness, nor of unity.
Knowing Self to be All, why does your mind choose to suffer?

5.11

In Brahman, concepts like good and evil do not exist,
nor do concepts like birth, living and dying.
There is only immaculate pure Being,
empty and infinite, like space.
Knowing Self to be All, why does your mind choose to suffer?

5.12

Being has no thoughts, no feelings, no knowledge, no knowing.
It desires nothing and wants for nothing.
It both does and does not exist. It is spontaneous potentiality —
the ever-pure, ever-free source and seed.
Knowing Self to be All, why does your mind choose to suffer?

5.13

Being is Truth, Truth is Being. 5.14
It is not sullied by ideas about reality and unreality,
unity and separateness. It both is and is not One.
Knowing Self to be All, why does your mind choose to suffer?

Being is Supreme. Its home is infinity, its family is all things. 5.15
Ideas about bondage and liberation,
ignorance and wisdom, do not occur Here.
Knowing Self to be All, why does your mind choose to suffer?

This universe of ever-changing phenomena is illusory, unreal. 5.16
That which is forever changeless is Reality.
This world of names and definitions is illusory, untrue.
That which is forever nameless and indefinable is Truth.
Knowing Self to be All, why does your mind choose to suffer?

There is only one Soul. 5.17
It pervades everywhere forever.
There is only one Life.
It lives all beings and things.
Knowing Self to be All, why does your mind choose to suffer?

To see difference in That which is undifferentiated is ignorance. 5.18
To imagine changes in That which never moves is senseless.
Here, there is only the infinite stillness of pure Awareness.
Knowing Self to be All, why does your mind choose to suffer?

In Brahman there are no states—no state of bondage, 5.19
no state of liberation, no state of virtue, no state of sin,
no state of wholeness, no state of emptiness.
Knowing Self to be All, why does your mind choose to suffer?

Being is not subject to notions like cause and effect, 5.20
color and no-color, caste and no-caste, unity and separateness.
Knowing Self to be All, why does your mind choose to suffer?

Self is omnipresent. Self indwells all beings and things, 5.21
though they are without reality and do not indwell Self.
Self is limitless pure Awareness, ever-free, ever-still.
Knowing Self to be All, why does your mind choose to suffer?

Brahman is Everything everywhere forever.
Brahman is No-Thing nowhere now.
It is pervasive and absent, immutable and ephemeral,
pure and manifest. There is no day or night.
Knowing Self to be All, why does your mind choose to suffer?

5.22

Bondage and liberation, unity and separation,
reasoning and intuition — the concept of opposites
does not hold sway in Brahman.
Knowing Self to be All, why does your mind choose to suffer?

5.23

Time and its divisions, like morning and evening, are denied.
Atoms and sub-particles are denied. The primordial elements
of earth, air, space, water and fire, are denied.
Ultimate Reality cannot be denied. It is Truth pure and simple.
Knowing Self to be All, why does your mind choose to suffer?

5.24

Self has no body or form, nor does it lack a body or form.
Self has no different states, like waking, dreaming and sleeping.
Self is forever nameless and observes no rules.
Knowing Self to be All, why does your mind choose to suffer?

5.25

Self is clear and vast like space.
Self pervades and transcends universe.
Self is always and everywhere the same.
Self is beyond reality, non-reality, and everything that changes.
Knowing Self to be All, why does your mind choose to suffer?

5.26

Self is indifferent to virtue and vice, wealth and poverty,
desire and aversion, substance and insubstantiality.
Knowing Self to be All, why does your mind choose to suffer?

5.27

Self knows nothing of grief and joy, pleasure and pain.
Self does not distinguish between teacher and disciple.
Knowing Self to be All, why does your mind choose to suffer?

5.28

Self never moves but is not immovable.
Self does not give birth to reality and illusion.
Self is not strong or weak, homogenous or diverse.
Knowing Self to be All, why does your mind choose to suffer?

5.29

Self is the quintessence of all elemental principles.   5.30
Activities in the phenomenal world are not real.
There is no division in Self.
Knowing Self to be All, why does your mind choose to suffer?

As the scriptures have said, the manifested world of earth,   5.31
people, universe and so on, is like water in a mirage.
Truly, Brahman alone exists, all-pervasive and never-ending.
Knowing Self to be All, why does your mind choose to suffer?

Where knowing cannot go, how can there be knowledge?   5.32
Supremely pure and free, absorbed in infinite bliss,
the Avadhuta spontaneously sings the song of Absolute Reality.

Chapter 6

As the scriptures have said in many ways,
the manifested world of earth, people, universe and so on,
is like water in a mirage.
Self alone exists! Limitless, eternal, all-encompassing.
To what can it be compared? And by whom?

6.1

In Self there is neither division nor unity,
neither action nor stillness.
Self alone exists! Limitless, eternal, all-encompassing.
Who is there to perform austerities and offer sacrifices?

6.2

Self is eternal and omnipresent, undivided, all-pervasive,
and without any dimension whatever.
Self is One. Self is Absolute.
Thoughts and words cannot touch it.

6.3

In Self there is no night or day, no rising or setting of suns.
Self alone exists! Limitless, eternal, all-encompassing.
How can there be sun and moon and fire to illuminate it?

6.4

In Self there are no concepts like action and inaction,
thought and no-thought, desire and no-desire.
Self alone exists! Limitless, eternal, all-encompassing.
How can there be notions of with and without?

6.5

Self has no essence, nor does it lack essence.
It is neither full nor empty, void nor manifested.
Self alone exists! Limitless, eternal, all-encompassing.
How can there be such as *first* and *last*, or *is* and *is-not*?

6.6

In Self there are no differences, nor is there non-difference.
There is no knower, no knowing, no thing to be known.
Self alone exists! Limitless, eternal, all-encompassing.
How can there be a third state of consciousness? Or a fourth?

6.7

All teachings are false.   6.8
All that is not taught is false.
What seems to be known is false.
What seems to be unknown is false.
Self alone exists! Limitless, eternal, all-encompassing.
How can there be senses, intellect, mind and objects?

Space and air are not real.   6.9
Earth and fire are not real.
Clouds and water are not real.
Self alone exists! Limitless, eternal, all-encompassing.
How can there be sky and oceans?

In Self there are no worlds or hells or heavens,   6.10
no imaginary gods.
Self alone exists. Limitless, eternal, all-encompassing.
How can there be notions of good and evil?

In Self there is no death or immortality,   6.11
no action nor inaction.
Self alone exists! Limitless, eternal, all-encompassing.
How could there be a *coming from* or *going to*?

There is no difference between matter and consciousness.   6.12
There is no such thing as *cause and effect*.
Self alone exists! Limitless, eternal, all-encompassing.
How can you speak of Self and not-Self?

There are no *gunas*, no stages of life.   6.13
Self alone exists! Limitless, eternal, all-encompassing.
How can there be infancy, youth or old age?

In Self there are no castes or stages,   6.14
no such thing as *agent and change*.
Self alone exists! Limitless, eternal, all-encompassing.
How can there be the perishable and the imperishable?

The destroyed and the undestroyed are both unreal.   6.15
The devourer and the devoured are false.
The creator and the created are One.
Self alone exists! Limitless, eternal, all-encompassing.
How can there be ideas of destruction or permanence?

In Self there is no man nor beast, no woman or eunuch,   6.16
no husband, wife or child.
Self alone exists! Limitless, eternal, all-encompassing.
How can there be vessels of pleasure and pain?

Self is absent of grief and sorrow, absent of delusion and doubt.   6.17
Self alone exists! Limitless, eternal, all-encompassing.
How can there be notions of *I* and *mine*?

Self is absent of ideas about vice and virtue,   6.18
of ideas about freedom and bondage.
Self alone exists! Limitless, eternal, all-encompassing.
How can there be sorrow or happiness?

There is no difference between the sacrificial rite   6.19
and the performer of the rite.
There is no difference between the objects being sacrificed
and the sacrificial fire.
Self alone exists! Limitless, eternal, all-encompassing.
How can there be actions and results of actions?

In Self there is no sorrow or joy, no pride or humility.   6.20
Self alone exists! Limitless, eternal, all-encompassing.
How can there be passion or dispassion?

In Self there is neither illusion nor absence of illusion.   6.21
There is no greed or generosity.
Self alone exists! Limitless, eternal, all-encompassing.
How can there be discrimination or non-discrimination?

There is no *you* nor *I*.   6.22
Stories about caste and family and race are lies.
I am the Absolute, the One Reality.
To what should I offer my devotion?

Concepts of teacher and disciple are absent.   6.23
There is no difference between instruction and reflection.
I am the Absolute, the One Reality.
To what should I offer my devotion?

There is no imagining of separate bodies, nor of illusory worlds.   6.24
Uncertainty and certainly are both unreal.
I am the Absolute, the One Reality.
To what should I offer my devotion?

Passion and dispassion are absent.   6.25
I am spotless, immovable, immaculate.
I am the Absolute, the One Reality.
To what should I offer my devotion?

There is no difference between body and no-body.   6.26
The apparent actions of life are not happening.
I am the Absolute, the One Reality.
To what should I offer my devotion?

Where knowing cannot go, how can there be knowledge?   6.27
Supremely pure and free, absorbed in infinite bliss,
the Avadhuta spontaneously sings the song of Absolute Reality.

Chapter 7

The Avadhuta wears castoff garments made of rags.   7.1
His path is free of virtue and vice.
He lives alone in a deserted place,
absorbed in the Oneness of Being.

The mark of the Avadhuta may or may not be visible.   7.2
Beyond right and wrong, he is nevertheless always honest.
His nature is pure Reality, immaculate Truth.
How can such a one engage in arguments and discussions?

The Avadhuta is free of the snares of hope and desire.   7.3
He has no need of purifying acts, and is not harnessed
by rules about acceptable behavior.
He is gloriously bereft of all things.
He has become That Which Is.

Having realized True Nature, how can the Avadhuta   7.4
say whether or not he has a body?
Whether or not he has passion or attachment?
He is Reality itself, clear and endless. He is unbounded Truth.

In the immaculate unchanging Absolute,   7.5
is there a preference between form and formless?
Between knowledge and no-knowledge?
My form is clear and empty like sky.
How is perception of objects possible?

Self is indivisible and boundless, like space.   7.6
Its nature is ever-pure and forever changeless.
How can there be division and separation?
How can there be bondage and liberation?
How can there be any changes whatever?

Everywhere there is one Absolute Truth,
one limitless Reality. How can there be separation and union?
The One is the All, unceasing.
How can there be notions of loss and gain,
weakness and strength, void and substance?

7.7

Everywhere there is one Absolute Truth,
pure, empty, infinite as space.
How can it be together or apart? Have color or no-color?
Be happy or unhappy? Have enemies or friends?

7.8

The Avadhuta may observe the precepts of yoga or he may not.
Even so, he is called a yogi.
He may have experiences and possessions or he may not.
Even so he enjoys.
He is free of enjoyment and non-enjoyment, therefore he enjoys.
He moves about serenely, his mind at rest in contentment.

7.9

If a practitioner of yoga believes in knowledge and ignorance,
duality and non-duality, how can he realize Truth?
How can he be dispassionate in life?
How can he enjoy the immensity of immaculate Oneness?

7.10

Self is infinite and boundless as sky.
It is uncreated and cannot be destroyed.
It is devoid of concepts like *whole* and *divided*,
like *hold on* and *let go*.
How can there be talk of true or false,
expansion or contraction, substance or void?
Self is the eternal auspicious moment.

7.11

Unattached to life and the world, the Avadhuta abides in Self.
He has transcended all things and is free of birth and death.
What does it matter if he meditates or not?

7.12

The world is made by magic.
It is nothing but illusion, a mirage in the desert.
Only the Absolute Self exists.

7.13

Avadhutas do not seek wealth and enjoyment,   7.14
nor do they seek righteousness or liberation.
We are indifferent to everything!
Only seekers are concerned with ideas about passion
and dispassion, attachment and non-attachment.

Where knowing cannot go, how can there be knowledge?   7.15
Supremely pure and free, absorbed in infinite bliss,
the Avadhuta spontaneously sings the song of Absolute Reality.

Chapter 8

Oh Brahman, by seeking you I have denied your omnipresence.   8.1
By contemplating you, I have denied your formless mystery.
By praising you, I have implied you are accessible to thought.
Forgive me for these three offenses.

One who is not agitated by desires,   8.2
whose senses are controlled, who is free of possessions,
who eats in moderation and covets nothing in the world,
who is gentle, pure, serene and steadfast,
who has taken refuge in Absolute Self —
such a one can be called a sage.

The sage is intelligent and insightful. He honors others.   8.3
He is farsighted, courageous, capable and resolute.
He has triumphed over mind and senses but takes no credit.
He is courteous, compassionate, and a good friend to have.

The sage is non-violent and kind-hearted.   8.4
He is innocent, gracious, merciful, forbearing.
He sees everyone as God and is good to all.
His soul has been released.
He is established in Truth.

The qualities of an Avadhuta,   8.5
and the meaning and essence of the syllables AH-VA-DHU-TA,
are known to teachers of Vedanta and the Vedas.

The quality of the sound "A" signifies   8.6
one who is free from the bondage of hope,
who is released from the idea of beginning, middle and end,
and who abides in perpetual contentment.

The quality of the sound "VA" indicates   8.7
one who has uprooted all desires, whose speech is uplifting,
and who lives always in the present moment.

The quality of the sound "DHU" signifies
one whose body is covered with dust,
whose mind is uncluttered by negative thoughts,
and who is beyond the need of meditation.

8.8

The quality of the sound "TA" indicates
one who is steadfast in Truth,
who does not suffer worries and desires,
and who is free of ignorance and egoism.

8.9

This song of the Avadhuta has been composed in joy
by Dattatreya.

8.10

Whoever realizes Self
upon reading or hearing this wisdom
is freed from the cycle of birth and death.

Om Tat Sat

Faith Mind Sutra
Hsin Hsin Ming

Seng Ts'an

Hsin Hsin Ming is one of the earliest and most influential Zen writings, containing both Buddhist and Taoist teachings. Sometimes referred to as the first Zen poem, it is attributed to Seng Ts'an, the Third Chinese Patriarch of Ch'an (Zen). Little is known about him, but one text records that he was a layman in his forties suffering from leprosy when he encountered Huike, the Second Patriarch, and was initiated into his order. Huike was impressed with this layman's grasp of the Way and named him Seng Ts'an, "Jewel of the Community." Gradually, Seng Ts'an was cured of his illness, and after only two years of practice Huike presented him with the robe and bowl signifying transmission of the Dharma.

Around that time began the persecution of Buddhists in China prophesied by Bodhidharma. Huike ordered his successor to hide in the mountains and not teach—an order he obeyed for twenty-four years, at one point feigning mental illness to escape execution. In the year 592, he met the monk Tao-hsin, who received transmission from Seng Ts'an and became the Fourth Patriarch. Seng Ts'an died in 606, reportedly standing erect under a large tree with his hands pressed together in *gassho*.

Hsin translates literally as "faith," but not in the sense of belief. Rather, the unshakeable certainty of faith that arises from the direct experience of Self, of Truth. The second *hsin* translates as "heart-mind," meaning not the ignorant ego-mind of the individual, but the Buddha Mind, the One Mind. *Ming* translates most closely as "inscription." but also connotes warnings or admonitions.

Tao is self-evident to one with no preferences.   1
When like and dislike are absent,
the Real is obvious and clear.
Make the slightest distinction, however,
and it appears disguised as heaven and earth.

If you wish to know Truth, hold no opinions.   2
To judge and choose is the disease of the mind.
When Truth goes un-observed,
the mind roils with self-centered striving.
No good can come of this.

Tao is immaculate, empty.   3
It lacks nothing, is nothing.
Desire and aversion blind you to Suchness.

Do not become entangled in outer life,   4
nor indulge in feelings of detachment.
Serenely abide in what is, and all such dualities disappear.

When you impose stillness to stop activity,   5
stillness becomes an activity.
When you prefer one thing to another, you cannot abide in One.
Not abiding in One, you are bound by both action and stillness.

Believing appearances are real, you cannot see their Source.   6
Seeing appearances are void, you see both Source and show.
The more you talk and think, the further astray you wander.
Stop thinking and talking and All becomes known.

Returning to Source, one finds refuge.   7
Pursuing appearances pulls you further away.
At the moment of enlightenment,
neither appearances nor emptiness are known.
Changes transpiring in an imaginary world
are visible only to ignorance.
Do not seek Truth. Just stop having opinions.

Do not remain mired in the dual-natured world.   8
Avoid pursuing its offerings.
Distinguishing even a trace of right and wrong,
of this and that, roots the mind in confusion.

The dual-natured world arises from One,   9
but do not cling to ideas of Oneness.
When the mind abides in Tao, the world cannot oppose it.
Without opposites, the world cannot exist.

When discriminating thoughts cease to arise, the mind vanishes.   10
When the mind vanishes, the world is seen as unreal.
When the world is seen as unreal,
the perceiver of the world cannot be found.

Objects appear as objects because the mind believes it is subject.   11
In truth, subject and object are not separate.
They arise as One from emptiness
and comprise the ten thousand things.
If you do not discriminate between coarse and fine,
how can preference and opinion arise?

Abiding in Tao is neither difficult nor easy — it simply is.   12
But those with limiting beliefs, fearful and indecisive,
waver constantly between eagerness and hesitation.
The faster they hurry, the slower they go.

There are no degrees of attachment.   13
Being attached even to the idea of enlightenment
preserves ignorance. Just let things be as they are.
All is Here. There is no coming or going.

Tao is your very nature.   14
Seeing this, everything is clear —
you walk free and undisturbed as Tao.

When you are tied to mind-thoughts,
everything is murky, confusing.
The tiresome habit of judging saps energy,
and makes peace of mind impossible.
What benefit is derived from imagining
distinctions and separations?

    15

If you wish to abide in Tao,
do not dislike the world you now experience.
Indeed, to see there is no difference
between Tao and world is enlightenment itself.
The wise man expends no effort.
The foolish man ties himself in knots.

    16

Tao is singular, solitary, indivisible.
Distinctions are the imaginings of ignorance.
To seek Truth in the endless maze
of the discriminating mind is a great mistake.

    17

Activity and stillness transpire only in illusion.
With enlightenment there is nothing to like or dislike.
The dual-natured world is a seeming, an inference,
a flowery dream in air. How foolish to try to hold it.
Loss and gain, right and wrong, coarse and fine...
Let it all go.

    18

If the eye never sleeps, dreaming stops.
When the mind ceases to discriminate,
the ten thousand things are seen to be of one Suchness.
To fathom Suchness is to be released from bondage.
When all things are seen as One, the timeless Self is Realized.
This state cannot be described. No analogies are possible.

    19

When movement stops, there is no movement.
When there is no movement, there is nothing to stop.
Both movement and rest disappear.
Without such dualities, Oneness itself cannot exist.
Nothing can be said about this ultimate condition.

    20

When mind becomes Mind abiding in Tao,
self-centered striving ceases.
Irresolution and doubt vanish. Life unfolds in Faith.
With a single stroke, bondage dissolves into freedom.
Nothing remains to hold on to.

All is Void. Empty, clear, self-illuminating — it makes no effort.
Thinking, feeling, imagining, knowing...
These things have no place Here.
In Suchness there is no self or other.

To come into harmony with Suchness,
see everything as "Not Two." In Not Two, nothing is separate,
nothing left out. In all places and times,
enlightenment means becoming this single Truth.

The Real is not bound by time or space.
Nothing defines it as large or small.
A single thought spins ten thousand years.
The thoughts of ten thousand years occur in a single moment.

Emptiness here, emptiness there, emptiness inside and out.
The universe in all its totality is thus arrayed before you.
Boundaries and definitions do not exist.
Infinitely large, infinitely small — no difference.
So too with existence and non-existence.
Don't waste time arguing, and denying the Real.

The One is all things. All things are the One.
Make no distinctions as you move about and mingle.
When enlightenment occurs,
worries about attainment and perfection vanish.
The Real cannot be divided.
Faith Mind and Source are Not Two.

Words! Tao is beyond words.
Yesterday never happened.
Tomorrow never will.
Today does not exist

Atma Shatakam

Atma Shatakam, also known as *Nirvana Shatakam*, is a famous Hindu poem that summarizes Advaita Vedanta philosophy in much the same way as the *Heart Sutra* summarizes Buddhist philosophy.

According to legend, the great mystic and scholar Adi Shankara (788-820 CE) was a young boy of eight wandering the Himalayas in search of a worthy guru when he met Swami Govindapada Acharya, who asked him: "Who are you?" The young Shankara replied with six spontaneously composed stanzas that have come to be known as the *Atma Shatakam*. They have since become an important source of contemplation for those seeking Self-realization.

The speaker in the poem is one who has realized his True Nature as God. Like the *Heart Sutra*, the *Atma Shatakam* lists all the many things that the speaker is not, then asserts the one thing he is:

I am Absolute Awareness of Unfathomable Love and Grace.
I am Shiva.

太上老君

1.

I am not the mind. I am not the intellect or intelligence.
I am not the ego, nor am I a deeper self or soul.
I am not the five sense organs—eyes, ears, nose, tongue and skin.
Nor am I the five elements—earth, air, water, fire and space.
I am Absolute Awareness of Eternal Love and Bliss.
I am Shiva.

2.

I am not energy alone, nor am I the five types of breath.
I am not the seven materials of the body—
blood, bone, muscle, marrow, fat, lymph and semen.
I am not the five bodily mechanisms—
speaking, grasping, breeding, mobility and elimination.
Nor am I the five veils obscuring True Nature—
the sheaths of body, energy, mind, intellect and pleasure.
I am Absolute Awareness of Eternal Love and Bliss.
I am Shiva.

3.

I have no hatred or desire, no likes or dislikes,
no attachments or aversions.
I have no greed or delusion, no arrogance or pride,
no jealousy or envy.
I have no duties, no money, no bondage, no liberation.
I am Absolute Awareness of Eternal Love and Bliss.
I am Shiva.

4.

I have no virtues or vices, no pleasure or pain,
no joy or sorrow, no good deeds or sins.
I have no need of scriptures, mantras, rituals, chanting,
sacrifices, or pilgrimages to holy places.
I am neither the observer nor that which is observed—
nor am I the process of observation.
I am Absolute Awareness of Eternal Love and Bliss.
I am Shiva.

5.
I do not fear death, nor is death possible for me.
I am not separate from True Self.
I have no caste or destiny. I never doubt or question my existence.
I have no father or mother, nor was I ever born.
I have no family or kin, no acquaintances or friends,
no teachers or disciples.
I am Absolute Awareness of Eternal Love and Bliss.
I am Shiva.

6.
I am void of attributes, form, and substance.
I have no attachment to the world, or to liberation from it.
I have no desires—I am All That Is, forever.
I pervade the far reaches of everywhere.

I am Absolute Awareness of Unfathomable Love and Grace.
I am Shiva.

Tao Te Ching
Lao Tsu

Probably the best known and most widely translated of the texts in this book, *Tao Te Ching* is the fundamental work of Taoism, and not only points with poetic elegance to the mystery of Oneness, but provides practical guidelines for cultivating character, conducting war, and governing nations.

As with most ancient texts, authorship is difficult to determine. It is commonly attributed to a specific person named Lao Tsu, who is said to have been a contemporary of Confucius, and may have been an archivist to the emperor. Some historians point out, however, that one meaning of the characters *lao tsu* is "old man," and that it was more likely a nickname than a proper name. These same two characters can also form the words "old scholar," pronounced *roshi* in Japanese — a title usually reserved for a Zen master.

Carrying out one's work in an unassuming manner is an important aspect of Taoist philosophy. So much so that often a Taoist writer or painter would either not sign his work, or use a pseudonym that honored his teacher. It is not a stretch, therefore, to surmise that the *Tao Te Ching* may well have been written by a sage — or sages — wishing to remain anonymous, as well as pay homage to the old masters who had come before.

The case for more than one author is a good one. There is a certain inconsistency in the poetics and content that suggest not only multiple writers but perhaps multiple time periods as well. Regardless, in the end only the work itself matters. The *Tao Te Ching* is a profound, enduring text that never ceases to amaze, mystify, inspire, and reveal. Whoever first brushed these verses on paper was merely the middle man. The words are from the Source.

One

That which can be perceived is not the timeless That.
That which can be named is not the nameless One.

The source of heaven and earth is without form or substance.
Naming creates the ten thousand things.

When desire is absent, Mystery is obvious.
When desire occurs, Creation unfolds.

Mystery and Creation arise from the same source.
The source is emptiness.
Void within Void.
The realm of Tao.

Two

Judging beauty creates ugliness.
Defining good creates evil.
All and Void arise together.

Hard and soft, long and short, high and low,
sound and silence, now and then.
Opposites exist because of each other.

Therefore the sage acts by not-doing and teaches no-thought.
The ten thousand things arise and vanish without him.
He works without motive, indifferent to outcome.
Because there is no doer, his actions are timeless.

Three

Bestowing honor breeds ambition.
Hoarding treasure invites thieves.
Displaying objects of desire sows the seeds of discontent.

Therefore the sage governs by emptying minds and filling bellies,
by weakening wills and strengthening bones.

He extols the virtue of desireless unknowing
and keeps intellects off balance.

When not-doing is accomplished, nothing remains undone.

Four

Tao is hollow emptiness.

The substance of All, it is absent of substance.
Dimensionless Void,
it is the source of the ten thousand things.

It blunts sharpness, unravels entanglements,
diffuses brightness, merges with dust.

Dark, invisible, it only seems to be.
It is the child of No-thing
and the father of God.

Five

The realm of heaven and earth is indifferent to the myriad creatures.
They appear as straw dogs.
The sage is indifferent to the multitudes of men.
They appear as straw dogs.

The realm of heaven and earth is like a bellows, both empty and full.
Moving, it brings forth, endlessly.

More words, less understanding.
Hold fast to the core.

Six

The urge of creation is ceaseless.
It is called the Dark Mother.

The womb of the Dark Mother
is the ground of heaven and earth.

Timeless, imperceptible, it continues ever-present.
Endless use does not touch it.

Seven

The realm of heaven and earth is everlasting.

Why is it everlasting?
Because it is not conscious of itself.
Having no thought of being, it never is not.

Like this, the sage forgets himself, so is always present.

Without self-concern, the self is eternal.
When self-interest subsides, fulfillment happens.

Eight

Supreme virtue is like water.
It nourishes the ten thousand things without effort
and flows in places men shun.
It is like Tao.

Stand on solid ground.
Go deep into the heart.
Speak only what is true.

In friendship, be kind.
In governing, be just.
In enterprise, be able.
In action, watch the timing.

Do not contend with nature and nothing will go wrong.

Nine

An over-filled cup is difficult to carry.
An over-sharp point is easily broken.

Fill your house with gold and jade
and it cannot be protected.
Become puffed with pride and disaster will follow.

Do only what needs doing then forget it.
This is the way of heaven.

Ten

While maintaining a body can you become One?
While breathing the force of life can you be innocent as a babe?

While polishing the dark mirror can you be without dust?
While loving and ruling the people can you refrain from action?

While coming and going from heaven
can you be passive as a woman?
Understanding all things can you abide in unknowing?

Give birth and nurture.
Create without claim.
Lead without taking command.
This is supreme virtue.

Eleven

Thirty spokes of the wheel converge to define a hole.
Clay is molded into pots to shape emptiness.
Walls are hammered into rooms to enclosed space.
Windows are cut into walls to frame absence.

Though things may have value,
without no-thing they are useless.

Twelve

The five colors confuse the eye.
The five tones deaden the ear.
The five flavors dull the palette.

Racing and hunting madden the mind.
Valuable goods hinder movement.

Therefore the sage is guided by his gut, not his senses.
He attends to one and ignores the other.

Thirteen

Receive honor with dismay.
Accept misfortune gratefully.

Why receive honor with dismay?
Honor and dishonor cause the same disturbance.
With honor comes the fear of disgrace.
With disgrace comes anxiety and dread.

Why accept misfortune gratefully?
Misfortune weakens the bond to body and self.
Without a separate self, what misfortune is possible?

See misfortune as a condition of separation
and you will become whole.
See the world as your body
and All will be delivered unto you.

Fourteen

Searching, we cannot see it. We call it ephemeral.
Straining, we cannot hear it. We call it ethereal.
Reaching, we cannot grasp it. We call it intangible.

These three are often confused because they are the same.

The One is not bright above and dark below.
Transparent, it moves in and out of nothing.

Its form has no shape.
Its image has no substance.
It is indistinct, elusive.

Nothing to face, nothing to follow.

Hold to the timeless Tao.
Abide in the present.
Now is the ancient beginning.

Fifteen

The old masters were deep, unfathomable,
profound beyond understanding.
Because they were unfathomable
we can only describe their demeanor.

Cautious, as if crossing an icy stream.
Alert, as if sensing danger.
Respectful, like visiting guests.
Yielding, like melting ice.
Simple, like uncarved wood.
Open, like beckoning valleys.
Mysterious, like opaque pools.

Still the mind and the mud settles.
Do nothing and action comes of itself.

One who embraces Tao has no desire for fulfillment.
Not desiring fulfillment,
he is finished with birth and death.

Sixteen

Be completely empty.
Be completely still.

Witness the ten thousand things
appear and vanish in one motion.
Watch as they arise, linger,
and return to the source — stillness.

This is the way it is.
It is called everlasting life.
To witness the everlasting is to be awake.

Not seeing the everlasting, one engages in blind action.
Blind action leads to misfortune.

Seeing the everlasting, one encompasses all.
Encompassing all, one is impartial.
Being impartial, one acts nobly.
Acting nobly, one enters heaven.

Entering heaven is to be one with Tao.
Being one with Tao is to be everlasting.

Though the body dies, nothing is disturbed.

Seventeen

When a sage governs, people barely notice.

Lesser rulers are praised and loved.
Lesser still are feared and obeyed.
The least are ridiculed and despised.

Trust is earned by trusting.

The sage uses words sparingly.
His work is done without fanfare.
People say: "It happened by itself."

Eighteen

When Tao is forgotten,
charity and righteousness are born.

When intelligence and knowledge are valued,
duplicity and pretense soon follow.

When the family is discordant,
love and duty are preached.

When the country is in chaos,
loyal patriots appear.

Nineteen

Abandon holiness, renounce wisdom.
It will be a hundred times better for everyone.

Eliminate morality and benevolence.
Love and empathy will naturally return.

Give up cleverness and profit.
Thieves and bandits will disappear.

But these are outward lessons, not the core.
Be simple. Be true.
Cast off selfhood and desire.

Twenty

Between yes and no, is there really much difference?
Good and bad, are they so far apart?
Must I think as others think?
Alas, there would be no end to fear.

The multitudes are busy with feasts and celebrations.
In spring they climb towers and enjoy the view.
I alone am unmoved, like an infant too young to smile.

Others have more than enough.
I alone have nothing.
My mind is that of a fool—empty.

Others are clear and bright.
I alone am nebulous and dim.
Others are alert and clever.
I alone am withdrawn, adrift in the ocean,
directionless as swirling wind.

Everyone else has purpose.
I alone am stubborn and untamed.
I am different.
I am nourished by the Dark Mother.

Twenty-One

Supreme virtue is to abide in Tao alone.

Tao is elusive and empty —
Oh yes, utterly empty and elusive —
yet within it dreamlike images arise.

Oh yes, it is indistinct and nebulous,
but within it shadows take form.

Oh yes, it is mysterious and dark,
but within it appearances originate.

The origin of Creation is the Real.
Its manifestations are unceasing.
This can be witnessed.

How do I witness the origin of Creation?
By looking!

Twenty-Two

Surrender and become whole.
Bend low and be straightened.
Become empty and be filled.
Burn out and be renewed.

Having nothing, beauty is revealed.
Having much, the way is hidden.

The sage abides in One
and thus is master of heaven and earth.
Not being self-absorbed, his vision is clear.
Not asserting himself, his light shines forth.
Not showing off, his merit is obvious.
Not praising himself, praise is showered upon him.
Not contending, nothing under heaven stands in his way.

This ancient saying, "Surrender and become whole,"
is it empty words?

Being whole means all things have returned to you.

Twenty-Three

To speak a short time is the way of nature.
High winds blow out before morning.
Hard rain subsides in a day.

What issues these?
The realm of heaven and earth.
If the realm of heaven and earth cannot maintain duration,
what chance has man?
This is why one aligns with Tao.

One who aligns with Tao is embraced by Tao.
He who lives a virtuous life attains Virtue.
One who loses his way feels lost.

He who is embraced by Tao becomes one with Tao.
One who attains Virtue enters heaven.
He who feels lost is ready for the Way.

Faith comes to the faithful.

Twenty-Four

He who stands on tiptoe is unsteady.
He who strides too hard cannot go far.

He who shines a light on himself is not enlightened.
He who asserts himself is not distinguished.
He who praises himself has no merit.
He who brags of his success will not last long.

Observers of Tao see these as spoiled food and pointless action—
shunned even by the myriad creatures.
One who knows Tao does not abide them.

Twenty-Five

Formless no-thing.
Precedent of heaven and earth.
Timeless, unchanging, solitary, silent.
It is the mother of the ten thousand things.

I do not know its name.
I call it Tao.
If forced to describe it,
I call it great.

Great implies vast reaches.
Vast reaches implies far away.
Far away implies return.

Tao is great.
Heaven is great.
Earth is great.
Man, too, is great.
In the realm there are four greats,
and a noble man is one.

Man follows the way of earth.
Earth follows the way of heaven.
Heaven follows the way of Tao.

Tao is the great Way.

Twenty-Six

Gravity is the ground of lightness.
Stillness is the master of unrest.

The sage can travel all day,
yet never wander far from the baggage wagon.
Though splendor and spectacle may beckon,
he remains unmoved, indifferent.

Why should the lord of ten thousand chariots act lightly?
One who acts lightly is not grounded.
One who is restless is not his own master.

Twenty-Seven

A good walker leaves no tracks.
A good speaker does not slip up.
A good accountant needs no counter.

A good doorsmith uses no bolts or locks
yet none can open what he closes.
A good binder uses no knots
yet what he binds cannot be unraveled.

The sage is good at saving souls and rejects no one.
He takes care of all things and abandons nothing.
This is called "the way of awareness."

The good man is the ignorant man's teacher.
The ignorant man is the good man's lesson.
To not honor the teacher and value the lesson —
no matter how much wisdom one acquires —
is to miss the mark.

This is an essential secret.

Twenty-Eight

Know the strength of the male, but keep to the role of the female.
Be the river of the world.
Being the river of the world, supreme virtue flows without end.
Flowing without end, you are the timeless infant.

Know the purity of light but maintain darkness.
Be the model of the world.
Being the model of the world, supreme virtue is constant.
Maintaining constant virtue, you are the boundless realm.

Be worthy of high honors, but keep to the role of the lowly.
Be the valley of the world.
Being the valley of the world, supreme virtue is fulfilled.
Being fulfilled, you are the uncarved block.

The uncarved block appears as separate things.
The sage sees things as they are and rules the world.

Great power does not divide.

Twenty-Nine

There are those who want to control the realm
and make it more to their liking.
They will never succeed.
The realm of heaven and earth is perfect, a sacred vessel.
It cannot be improved.
He who tries to change it, destroys it for himself.
He who tries to hold it, loses all contact.

It is natural for beings to sometimes lead, sometimes follow,
sometimes breathe hot, sometimes blow cold.
sometimes expand, sometimes decay,
sometimes overcome, sometimes collapse.

The sage therefore abandons pleasure, judgment, and pride.

Thirty

When counseling rulers, observers of Tao do not advise force.
This is certain to bring consequences.
Where great armies have passed, thorn bushes thrive.
Famine follows in the wake of war.
A good ruler does only what is necessary to achieve results.
He does not abuse position.

Achieve results, but do not glory in them.
Achieve results, but do not boast.
Achieve results, but be not proud.

Achieve results because there is no choice.
Achieve results, but do not overpower.
Doing more than necessary brings exhaustion.
This is not in harmony with Tao.

What is not in harmony with Tao soon perishes.

Thirty-One

Even the finest weapons are instruments of ill omen,
hated and feared by all creatures.
Observers of Tao have no use for them.

At home, a man of virtue gives precedence to the left.
At war, he gives precedence to the right.

Weapons are not the tools of a man of virtue.
Weapons are instruments of fear,
to be employed as a last resort.
Do not relish their use or admire their excellence.

To see weapons as excellent is to relish killing.
If you relish killing you will never find the Way.

On joyful occasions, precedence is given to the left.
On sad occasions, precedence is given to the right.

When an army is arrayed, the general is placed on the left.
The commander-in-chief is placed on the right.
Thus, war is conducted as a funeral rite.

When multitudes are being killed,
hold in your heart only sorrow.
When victory is achieved, mark it with mourning.

Thirty-Two

Tao is the uncarved block.
Timeless, undefined, infinitesimally subtle.
None is its master.

If lords and princes observed it,
the ten thousand things would arrive as guests to the table.
Heaven and earth would rejoice and sweet nectar would fall,
though none under heaven had decreed it.

When the whole is divided the parts are named.
There are already too many names.
It is time to stop. Knowing when to stop avoids exhaustion.

Tao in the world is like stream flowing to river flowing to sea.

Thirty-Three

One who knows others is wise.
One who knows self is enlightened.
One who masters others is strong.
One who masters self is powerful.

Knowing you have enough is fulfillment.
Exerting strong effort brings exhaustion.

He who abides where he is lasts long.
He who dies without ceasing is timelessly present.

Thirty-Four

Great Tao flows everywhere,
left and right, all directions.

The ten thousand things depend on it and it does not turn away.
Its purpose is fulfilled but it lays no claim.

It clothes and nourishes the ten thousand things but is not their lord.
It desires nothing.
It is smaller than small.

The ten thousand things return to it but it is not their master.
It is indeed great.
Because it knows nothing of greatness, it is greater than great.

Thirty-Five

Extol the great illusion and the men of the world will gather.
Talk of success, security, happiness and the multitudes will flock.
Offer music and tasty food and travelers will stop in.

Talk of Tao has no flavor.

Look for it—there is nothing to see.
Listen for it—there is nothing to hear.
Merge with it—there is no boundary or end.

Thirty-Six

If you want it to contract, let it expand.
If you want it to weaken, let it gain strength.
To bring a thing down, let it be raised high.
To bring a thing to you, let go.

This is called "perceiving the subtle workings."

Soft and weak overcome hard and strong.
A fish should not leave deep water.
A country should not show off its power.

Thirty-Seven

Tao does nothing yet nothing remains undone.

When a noble man observes this
the ten thousand things are transformed.
When the desire to act re-emerges,
it is stilled by the nameless no-thing.

Without things there is no desire.
Without desire there is stillness.
In stillness, the realm of heaven and earth is perfect.

Thirty-Eight

The man of high virtue is not aware of himself
and thus attains supreme virtue.
The man of low virtue self-consciously strives
and thus is without virtue.

The wise man does nothing
yet leaves nothing undone.
The ignorant man is consumed by doing
yet little is accomplished.

The compassionate man acts without motive.
The righteous man acts to gain merit.
The moral man acts to impose order.
If no one responds, he bares his arms and becomes an enforcer.

When Tao is lost there is virtue.
When virtue is lost there is goodness.
When goodness is lost there is morality.
When morality is lost, rules of conduct are imposed.

Rules are the remnants of trust and the beginning of chaos.
Knowledge is an ornamental blossom of Tao
and the beginning of misunderstanding.

The sage dwells in the depths not the surface,
in the root not the flower.
He abides in one and lets go of the other.

Thirty-Nine

Before time, these ancestors arise from One:

Heaven arises from One and becomes clear.
Earth arises from One and becomes firm.
Spirit arises from One and becomes divine.

Emptiness arises from One and becomes Creation.
The ten thousand things arise from One and become manifest.
Kings and princes arise from One and become exalted.

One is the source of All.

Separated from the Source:
the clearness of heaven would vanish,
the firmament of earth would dissolve,
the divinity of spirit would dissipate,
and Creation would become desolation.
The ten thousand things would perish,
and kingdoms would disappear.

Humility is the root of honor.
Lowliness is the foundation of esteem.

Thus, a noble man considers himself orphaned, bereft, unworthy.
This is knowing the humble source, is it not?

To seek praise is not praiseworthy.
Do not jangle like jewelry.
Be still as stone.

Forty

Tao moves by returning and acts by yielding.
Thus, the ten thousand things arise into being.

Being arises from non-being.
Things arise from no-thing.

Forty-One

When the wise student hears of Tao
he practices diligently.
When the average student hears of Tao
he practices off and on.
When the foolish student hears of Tao
he laughs out loud.
If the foolish do not laugh, it is not Tao.

Thus it is said:
The path of light is through darkness.
The road ahead leads back.
The easy way is most difficult.
The highest fulfillment is emptiness.

True purity seems sullied.
True abundance seems bereft.
True power seems weak.
True substance seems hollow.

The greatest region has no boundaries.
The best tools are fashioned slowly.
The highest sounds are hard to hear.
The perfect form has no shape.

Tao is unseen, undefined.
Yet Tao alone nourishes and brings all things to fulfillment.

Forty-Two

From Tao, One arises.
From One, two.
From two, three.
Three becomes the ten thousand things.

The ten thousand things carry yin on their backs
and hold yang in their arms.
Existence depends on the two.

Men hate to be orphaned, bereft, unworthy,
yet this is how the noble man describes himself.
Loss is gain, gain is loss.

I teach what has always been taught:
"A fervent man is surprised by death."
I see this as the foundation of my teaching.

Forty-Three

Under heaven, the soft and yielding
overcomes the hard and strong.
That without substance permeates the impenetrable.

Thus, I embrace non-action,
teach without words, work without doing.

Few under heaven understand this.

Forty-Four

Name or body, which is more precious?
Person or possessions, which is more dear?
Gain or loss, which is more harmful?

Excessive desire incurs great expense.
One who hoards treasure suffers loss.

One who knows enough is enough
will always have enough.
One who knows when to stop avoids exhaustion.
Thus, he will endure.

Forty-Five

Perfection appears imperfect but has no flaw.
Fulfillment appears as emptiness but has no limit.

Great truth is a paradox.
Great wisdom is self-evident.
Great eloquence is unpracticed.

Movement overcomes cold.
Tranquility overcomes heat.
Stillness and simplicity put all things right under heaven.

Forty-Six

When Tao is embraced in the realm,
race horses haul their own manure.
When Tao is unknown in the realm,
war horses are bred at the borders.

There is no greater curse than desire,
no greater misfortune than greed.

He who knows enough is enough,
will always have enough.

Forty-Seven

Without leaving home you can know the whole world.
Without looking out you can see heaven.

Seeking afar does not find what is near.

Thus, the sage knows without learning,
sees without seeking,
acts without doing.

Forty-Eight

For students of knowledge, every day something is acquired.
For observers of Tao, every day something falls away.

Less and less is done until not-doing is achieved.
When there is no doer, nothing remains to be done.

The realm of heaven and earth
is ruled by timeless principles.
He who tries to interfere is not ready to receive it.

Forty-Nine

The sage has no heart or mind of his own.
Thus, he knows the heart and mind of all.

I am good to the good
and good to the not-so-good.
This is the goodness of Virtue.

I trust the trustworthy
and have faith in those who should not be trusted.
This is the faith of Virtue.

The sage is in harmony with the realm of heaven and earth.
His mind is merged with the world.
People turn to him and listen.
He treats them as his children.

Fifty

In the passage from womb to grave,
one in three are disciples of living.
One in three are disciples of death.
One in three are just passing through.

All believe they have life.

He who knows the truth of existence
does not fear wild bulls or tigers.
He wears no armor in battle.

Bulls have no place to thrust their horns.
Tigers have no place to sink their claws.
Weapons have no place to enter.

Why is this?
Because death is for the living.

Fifty-One

Tao gives them life.
Virtue gives them nourishment.
The manifest world gives them form.
The tendencies of each make them what they are.

Therefore the ten thousand things honor Tao and esteem Virtue.
This honor and esteem are not commanded.
It is just the nature of things.

And so, all things arise from Tao.
By Virtue they are nourished, developed, clothed,
sheltered, soothed, aged, and buried.

To create without possessing,
to act without making claims,
to lead without taking command —
this is timeless Virtue.

Fifty-Two

Where the realm of heaven and earth begins
could be called the Mother of Creation.

Knowing the mother, become the child.
Being the child, stay close to the mother.
Death will not bother you.

Stay quiet, keep inside,
and you will never want for anything.
Open your mouth, meddle in affairs,
and you are beyond rescue.

Perceiving the subtle is insight.
To yield requires strength.
Use the light of Creation to become illuminated
and thus be saved.

This is called "entering the Absolute."

Fifty-Three

If I have the least bit of knowledge
I will follow the great Way alone
and fear nothing but being sidetracked.
The great Way is simple but people delight in complexity.

The government is corrupt.
The fields are overgrown. The granaries are empty.
Yet some wear fine clothes, carry sharp swords,
gorge on food and drink, and are surrounded by luxury.
They are thieves.

This is certainly not the great Way.

Fifty-Four

What is deeply rooted will not topple.
What is firmly grasped will not slip away.
It will be honored through generations of ancestors.

Cultivated in the self, Virtue is manifest.
Cultivated in the family, Virtue grows.
Cultivated in the village, Virtue flourishes.
Cultivated in the nation, Virtue abounds.
Cultivated in the universe, Virtue is everything.

As the self, observe the self.
As the family, observe the family.
As the village, observe the village.
As the nation, observe the nation.
As the universe, observe the universe.

How do I know the universe?
Like this.

Fifty-Five

A man of Virtue can be compared to a newborn child.

Snakes and scorpions do not strike him.
Fierce beasts do not prey upon him.
Birds of prey do not attack him.

Though his bones are soft and his muscles weak,
his grip is firm.
Without knowing the union of man and woman,
his organ stands erect.

His vital force is strong.
He can scream all day without becoming hoarse.
His harmony is perfect.

To know harmony is to know the everlasting.
To know the everlasting is enlightenment.

To interfere with life is ill-fated.
To control the breath causes strain.
If you exert yourself you will become exhausted.
This is not in harmony with Tao.

What is not in harmony with Tao does not long endure.

Fifty-Six

One who knows does not talk about it.
One who talks about it does not know.

Stay quiet.
Keep inside.
Blunt sharpness.
Unravel entanglements.
Diffuse brightness.
Merge with dust.

This is called "discovering original nature."

One who knows original nature is
indifferent to intimacy and estrangement,
unconcerned with benefit and harm,
immune to honor and disgrace.

He is embraced by heaven.

Fifty-Seven

Rule the country with sincerity.
Wage war with cunning.
Master the universe with indifference.

How do I know this is the way it is?

Because of this:
The more taboos, the poorer the people's spirit.
The sharper men's weapons, the more trouble in the land.
The greater the ingenuity, the more clutter in the world.
The more abundant the laws, the more abundant the thieves.

Therefore the sage says:
I take no action and the people naturally reform.
I remain at peace and the people become content.
I do not meddle and the people become prosperous.
I desire nothing and the people return to original nature.

Fifty-Eight

When government does not interfere, the people are genuine.
When government intrudes, the people are cunning.

Happiness is founded on misery.
Misery lurks within happiness.
Is there an end to it?
Nothing stays the same.

Honesty moves with deceit, good flows with evil,
but people's delusion persists.

Thus, the sage is sharp but not divisive,
straightforward but not hurtful,
principled but not severe,
illumined but not blinding.

Fifty-Nine

In leading people and serving heaven, nothing surpasses humility.
Humility is having no preferences.
Humility accumulates virtue.

Where virtue accumulates, nothing is impossible.
When nothing is impossible, there are no limits.
A man without limits is fit to rule the realm.
The mother of the realm is everlasting.

This is called being deeply rooted.
Timeless awareness of Tao.

Sixty

Governing a country is like cooking a delicate fish.

Rule in observance of Tao
and the forces of adversity become harmless.
They do not lose their power, only their power to harm.

The sage, too, does no harm and so he is not harmed.
Virtue flows unimpeded.

Sixty-One

A country becomes great by lying low, like the delta of a great river.
The confluence of the realm.
The mother of the world.

The female conquers the male by stillness.
Being still, she takes the lower position.

A great country conquers a small country
by taking the lower position.
A small country conquers a great country
by merging with it.

Thus, the great country conquers by yielding,
the small country conquers by being absorbed.

The great country needs more people.
The small country needs greater purpose.
Each gets what it needs.

It is proper for greatness to yield.

Sixty-Two

Tao is the ground of the ten thousand things.
It is the refuge of the good man
and the guardian of the bad.

Fine speech can buy high rank.
Good deeds can earn respect.
Should one without them be abandoned?

Therefore, on the day the son is crowned
and the three ministers named,
do not send gifts of jade and teams of horses.
Remain still and offer Tao.

Why has Tao been honored since ancient times?
"Seek and you shall find, transgress and you will be forgiven."
Is this not the reason?

Above all else, observe Tao.

Sixty-Three

Perform not-doing.
Work without motive.
Savor what has no flavor.

Regard the small as great, the few as many.
Repay injury with compassion.

See simplicity in the complex.
See greatness in small gestures.
Confront the difficult while easy.
Do great things in small increments.

The sage does nothing great,
but great things are accomplished.

Easy promises are easily broken.
Things taken lightly become difficult.
The sage regards nothing lightly,
therefore nothing is difficult.

Sixty-Four

That which is still is easy to contain.
What has not yet begun is easy to prevent.
The fragile is easily broken.
The minute is easily dispelled.

See things before they emerge.
Attend to them before they grow out of control.

A tree trunk that fills a man's arms
begins as a tiny shoot.
A terrace nine stories high
begins with a basket of dirt.
A journey of a thousand miles begins underfoot.

Those who strive meet defeat.
Those who grasp lose their grip.
The sage does nothing and never fails.
He has nothing and never loses.

Failure often comes on the verge of success.
Be as careful in the end as the beginning
and there will be no failure.

The sage desires no-desire.
He does not value wealth.
He learns by not thinking.
He restores to others what has been lost.

He helps the ten thousand things return to original nature
but does not interfere.

Sixty-Five

The ancient observers of Tao did not teach it to others.
They let them remain simple and unknowing.
People are difficult to deal with when they think they know.

Leaders who think they know are a curse to those they lead.
Leaders with a simple heart are a blessing to all.

Both are manifestations of the Source.
Knowing the Source is Virtue.
Virtue is mysterious, profound, far reaching.
Reaching far, it returns to itself and is complete.

Sixty-Six

Rivers rule valleys and seas rule rivers
because they take the lower position.

The sage is elevated by placing himself below others.
He leads by leaving himself behind.

When he assumes high position,
the people do not feel his weight.
When he rules they do not feel threatened.
The realm rejoices and never tires of his presence.

Because he does not contend,
nothing stands against him.

Sixty-Seven

Everyone agrees the Tao I teach is great,
yet unlike anything else.
Indeed, if it were not singular it would not endure.

I hold three treasures close:
The first is unconditional regard for all.
The second is being content with little.
The third is not placing myself before others.

From compassion comes courage.
From contentment comes an open heart.
From humility comes the capacity to lead.

Daring without mercy, charity without generosity,
ruling without modesty — this is the way of death.

Attacking with compassion, you are victorious.
Defending with compassion, you are impregnable.

What heaven favors it infuses with compassion.

Sixty-Eight

A good general is not aggressive.
A good warrior is not wrathful.

A skillful conqueror does not instigate battle.
A skillful employer serves those under him.

This is the virtue of not contending.
This is mastering the strength of others.

This is being in accord with the principles of heaven.

Sixty-Nine

Skillful warriors have a saying:
"Do not move first, play the guest.
Do not move forward an inch, retreat a foot."

This is called advancing without moving.
Reaching without showing one's arms.
Capturing without attacking.
Doing battle without weapons.

There is no greater mistake than underestimating the enemy.
Underestimating the enemy,
I risk losing everything of value.

Thus, when equal opponents are matched,
the one aware of sorrow will prevail.

Seventy

What I teach is easy to understand and practice,
yet no one understands it or puts it to practice.

My words are from the Source.
My actions are those of the ancestor.
People do not understand this.
Therefore, they do not understand me.

Those who see me as I am are rare.
Those who seek to follow my teachings are few.

The sage wears coarse clothing
but carries jade in his pockets.

Seventy-One

To know that you do not know is clarity.
To think that you know is sickness.

Being sick of sickness, one attains clarity.
The sage is sick of sickness.
Therefore, he is clear.

Seventy-Two

When people do not respect power,
disaster is on the horizon.

Do not limit their space.
Do not disrupt their lives.
Do not oppress them and they will not tire of you.

The sage knows himself, but does not claim knowledge.
He loves himself, but does not feel important.
He lets go of that and chooses this.

Seventy-Three

A courageous and reckless man will kill or be killed.
A courageous and careful man preserves life.
Of the two, which is beneficial and which brings harm?
Who knows what heaven favors—even the sage is unsure.

The way of heaven does not contend, yet overcomes.
Does not speak, yet converses.
Without being summoned it comes of its own,
unhurried, and according to plan.

The net of heaven is vast.
Though the mesh is wide, nothing slips through.

Seventy-Four

If people are not afraid of death,
why threaten them with death?

If people are in constant fear of death, and if being unruly
means you will be killed, who would dare be unruly?
Who would dare kill him?

There is always a Lord of Death.
Trying to do his job is like taking the place of an artisan.
He who tries to carve like a master carpenter
rarely avoids being cut.

Seventy-Five

Why are the people starving?
The government takes their grain for taxes.
Therefore they are starving.

Why are the people rebellious?
The government interferes in their lives.
Therefore they are rebellious.

Why do people ignore the gravity of death?
They are consumed by the intensity of life.
Therefore they ignore the gravity of death.

One who is not consumed by life
is better off than one who values it.

Seventy-Six

A man is born supple and soft.
At death he is rigid and hard.

The ten thousand things, the grass, the trees,
while living are tender and pliant.
In death they are dry and withered.

The hard and unbending are companions of death.
The soft and yielding are companions of life.

Thus, an inflexible army is easily defeated.
An unbending tree is easily broken.

The hard and strong are laid low.
The soft and yielding are raised up.

Seventy-Seven

The way of heaven, is it not like the stringing of a bow?
The high end is lowered, the low is raised up.
If the string is too long it is shortened.
If the string is too short it is lengthened.

The way of heaven takes from the excessive
and gives to the insufficient.
The way of man is different.
Those with too much take from those who have little.

Who keeps just enough and gives the rest to the world?
Only observers of Tao.

The sage works without expectation,
achieves without taking credit.
He does not desire to seem worthy.

Seventy-Eight

In all the world nothing is softer and weaker than water.
Yet for overcoming the hard and strong it is unequaled.

The pliant overcomes the unbending.
The submissive overcomes the unyielding.
Everyone knows this but no one puts it into practice.

Therefore the sage says:
He who takes on the suffering of the world is fit to rule it.
One who accepts the evils of the world as his own
is a king under heaven.

Truth is often a paradox.

Seventy-Nine

When bitter quarrels are settled, enmity is sure to remain.
What can be done?

A man of virtue pays his debts but does not exact his due.
He fulfills his obligations but makes no demands.

The Tao of heaven plays no favorites.
It flows with Virtue.

Eighty

Let the state be small.
Let the people be few.
Though they have equipment to arm ten battalions
they do not do it.
They take death seriously and do not venture far.

They have ships and carts
but there is no place they want to go.
They have armor and weapons
but they are not displayed.

Men return to knotting rope.
They enjoy their meals and are comfortable in their clothes.
They are content in their homes and happy with their lives.

Though the neighboring state is so close
you can hear the cocks and dogs,
they leave each other in peace as they grow old and die.

Eighty-One

Truth is not eloquent.
Eloquence is not truth.
Wise men do not try to persuade.
Whoever tries to persuade is not wise.

One who knows, claims unknowing.
One who claims knowledge, does not know.

The sage does not acquire.
He bestows what he has on others and always has more.
The more he gives, the greater his abundance.

The way of heaven is to give without harm.
The way of the sage is to serve without striving.

Bibliography

The following translations have informed and inspired the versions in this book. For all, I am immensely grateful.

Yoga Sutras

Beck, Sanderson: Yoga Sutras Union Threads
BonGiovanni: The Yoga Sutras of Patanjali—The Threads of Union
Hartranft, Chip: The Yoga-Sutra of Patanjali
Iyengar: Light on the Yoga Sutras of Patanjali
Johnston, Charles: The Yoga Sutras of Patanjali
Messenger, Chester: Yoga Sutras of Patanjali
Prabhavananda, Swami and Christopher Isherwood: How to Know God—The Yoga Aphorisms of Patanjali
Sarbatoare, Octavian: Yoga Aphorisms of Patanjali
Satchidananda, Sri Swami: The Yoga Sutras of Patanjali
Stiles, Mukunda: Yoga Sutras of Patanjali—With Great Respect and Love
Venkatesananda, Swami: Patanjali's Vision of Oneness—An Interpretive Translation
Vivekananda, Swami: The Yoga Sutras of Patanjali—The Essential Yoga Texts for Spiritual Enlightenment
Woods, James Haughton: The Yoga Sutras of Patanjali

Ashtavakra Gita

Balsekar, Ramesh: A Duet of One—The Ashtavakra Gita Dialogue
Byrom, Thomas: The Heart of Awareness—A Translation of the Ashtavakra Gita
Chinmayananda, Swami: Ashtavakra Gita
Nityaswarupananda, Swami: Ashtavakra Samhita
Richards, John: Ashtavakra Gita
Schoch, Manuel: Bitten by the Black Snake—The Ancient Wisdom of Ashtavakra
Sri Ramanasramam: Ashtavakra Gita

Dhammapada

Bhikkhu, Thanissaro: The Dhammapada
Buddharakkhita, Acharya: The Dhammapada—The Buddha's Path of Wisdom
Byrom, Thomas: Dhammapada
Carter, John Ross, and Mahinda Palihawadana:
Cleary, Thomas: Dhammapada—The Sayings of Buddha
Easwaran, Eknath: The Dhammapada
Fronsdal, Gil: The Dhammapada—A New Translation of the Buddhist Classic
Larkin, Geri: The Still Point Dhammapada—Living the Buddha's Essential Teachings
Maitreya, Balangoda Ananda and Thich Nhat Hanh: The Dhammapada
Mascaro, Juan: The Dhammapada
Müller, Friedrich Max: Wisdom of the Buddha—The Unabridged Dhammapada
Sangharakshita: Dhammapada—The Way of Truth
Wallis, Glenn: The Dhammapada—Verses on the Way

Book of Yeshua

Marshall, Bart: Christ Sutras: The Complete Sayings of Jesus from All Sources Arranged as Sermons

Heart Sutra

Buddhist Text Translation Society: The Heart Sutra
Conze , E.: The Heart Sutra
Dalai Lama and Thupten Jinpa: Essence of the Heart Sutra
Dragon Flower Ch'an Temple: The Heart Sutra
Ginsberg, Allen: The Heart Sutra
Hanh, Thich Nhat: The Heart of Understanding—Commentaries on the Prajnaparamita Heart Sutra
Hurtz, Leon: The Heart Sutra
Huy, Tru: The Heart Sutra
Larson, Eric: The Heart Sutra

Patton, Charles: The Heart Sutra
Pevahouse, Jerry: The Heart Sutra
Pine, Red: The Heart Sutra
Roach, Michael: The Heart Sutra
To, Lok: The Heart Sutra

Three Books of the Absolute

Rose, Richard: The Albigen Papers

Avadhuta Gita

Ashokananda, Swami: Avadhuta Gita of Dattatreya
Chetanananda, Swami: Avadhuta Gita of Dattatreya
Mal, Kannoo: The Avadhuta Gita of Dattatreya
Anonymous: The Avadhuta Gita by Dattatreya
Shastri, Hari Prasad: Avadhuta Gita by Dattatreya
Anonymous: Avadhuta Gita, Ever Free

Faith Mind Sutra (Hsin Hsin Ming)

Anonymous: Affirming Faith in Mind
Blythe, Robert: Hsin Hsin Ming
Clarke, Richard: Hsin Hsin Ming—Verses on the Faith Mind
Cleary, Thomas: Trust in the Heart
Humphreys, Christmas: On Trust in the Heart
Kwang, Hae: Hsin Hsin Ming—Trust Mind Inscription
Lombardo, Stanley: Hsin Hsin Ming—Trusting in Mind
Mitchell, Steven: The Mind of Absolute Trust
Olsen, Robert: Hsin Hsin Ming—The Mind of Absolute Trust
Osho: Hsin Hsin Ming—Discourses on Verses on the Faith-Mind
Pajin, Dusan: Hsin Hsin Ming—On Faith in Mind
Putkonen, Eric: Hsin Hsin Ming—Verses on the Perfect Mind
Suzuki, D.T.: Inscribed On the Believing Mind
Watson, Burton: Inscription on Trust in the Mind
Yen, Sheng: Faith in Mind—A Commentary on Seng Ts'an's Classic

Atma Shatakam

Anonymous: Multiple unattributed translations

Tao Te Ching

Addiss, Stephen and Stanley Lombardo: Tao Te Ching
Bynner, Witter: The Way of Life According to Lao Tzu
Chen, Ellen: Tao Te Ching
Feng, Gia-Fu and Jane English: Tao Te Ching
Henricks, Robert: Te-Tao Ching
Lau, D.C.: Tao Te Ching
Legee, James: Tao Te Ching
Le Guin, Ursula: Tao Te Ching — A Book About the Way and the Power of the Way
Mair, Victor: Tao Te Ching
Martin, William: Tao Te Ching — A Path and a Practice
Mitchell, Stephen: Tao Te Ching
Pine, Red: Lao-tzu's Taoteching — With Selected Commentaries of the Past 2000 Years
Star, Jonathan: Tao Te Ching — The Definitive Edition
Wu, John C.H.: Tao Teh Ching